Multinational Enterprises and Transparent Tax Reporting

This book examines tax transparency as part of multinational enterprises' corporate social responsibility (CSR). It considers revelations like the Panama and Paradise Papers that shed light on corporations' tax practices and the growing public dissatisfaction, resulting in legislative projects, such as the Organisation for Economic Co-operation and Development (OECD) base erosion and profit shifting. Tax transparency is defined as companies' voluntary disclosure of numerical tax data (e.g. taxes paid by country) and other tax-related information (e.g. tax policies). It is set apart from tax avoidance and tax evasion to clarify the often-blurred concepts.

In this book, tax transparency is placed in a historical context and possible drivers and hindering factors to tax transparency are investigated. Tax transparency is discussed in the light of socio-economic theories (stakeholder, legitimacy, institutional theory and reputation risk management), as well as economic theories (agency theory, signalling, proprietary costs) and information overload theory. The book provides examples of tax transparency development of the largest multinational enterprises in five countries (France, Germany, UK, Finland and USA) in six years, 2012–2017, a period featuring increased media coverage of tax matters and legislative movement in the OECD and the European Union. The future of tax transparency is discussed in light of quality characteristics, assurance of information and potential use of artificial intelligence.

Companies' managers and tax and CSR specialists benefit from the book by gaining insight into how to design transparent, high-quality tax reporting. Assurance professionals can use information about the quality criteria of tax transparency. Regulators can track historical development and see examples of voluntary tax transparency in companies' reporting. Scholars and students obtain theoretical framework for analysing the tax transparency phenomenon and the ability to distinguish between the concepts of tax transparency, planning, avoidance and evasion.

Alexandra Middleton is an assistant professor with a PhD in financial accounting from the University of Oulu, Finland. Her research interests include tax transparency, CSR and sustainable business development in the Arctic.

Jenni Muttonen is an assurance professional working in financial and sustainability audits. She holds a master of science in economics and business administration from the University of Oulu, Finland, and a master of arts in international relations from the University of St Andrews, UK.

Routledge Studies in Accounting

27 Interventionist Management Accounting Research
Theory Contributions with Societal Impact
Jouni Lyly-Yrjänäinen, Petri Suomala, Teemu Laine, and Falconer Mitchell

28 Accounting, Innovation and Inter-Organisational Relationships
Martin Carlsson-Wall, Håkan Håkansson, Kalle Kraus, Johnny Lind, and Torkel Strömsten

29 A History of Corporate Financial Reporting
John Richard Edwards

30 Public Sector Accounting, Governance and Accountability
Experiences from Australia and New Zealand
Edited by Robyn Pilcher and David Gilchrist

31 Managerial Accountant's Compass
Research Genesis and Development
Gary R. Oliver

32 Institutions and Accounting Practices after the Financial Crisis
International Perspective
Edited by Victoria Krivogorsky

33 Corporate Environmental Reporting
The Western Approach to Nature
Leanne J Morrison

34 Cost Management for Nonprofit and Voluntary Organisations
Zahirul Hoque and Tarek Rana

35 Multinational Enterprises and Transparent Tax Reporting
Alexandra Middleton and Jenni Muttonen

For a full list of titles in this series, please visit www.routledge.com/Routledge-Studies-in-Accounting/book-series/SE0715

Multinational Enterprises and Transparent Tax Reporting

Alexandra Middleton
and Jenni Muttonen

Routledge
Taylor & Francis Group
LONDON AND NEW YORK

First published 2020 by Routledge

2 Park Square, Milton Park, Abingdon, Oxon OX14 4RN
605 Third Avenue, New York, NY 10017

Routledge is an imprint of the Taylor & Francis Group, an informa business

First issued in paperback 2021

Publisher's Note

The publisher has gone to great lengths to ensure the quality of this reprint but points out that some imperfections in the original copies may be apparent.

British Library Cataloguing-in-Publication Data
A catalogue record for this book is available from the British Library

Library of Congress Cataloging-in-Publication Data
A catalog record for this book has been requested

ISBN: 978-0-8153-7256-1 (hbk)
ISBN: 978-1-03-217571-3 (pbk)
DOI: 10.4324/9781351245159

Typeset in Times New Roman
by Apex CoVantage, LLC

Alexandra Middleton: To my family

Jenni Muttonen: To my parents

Contents

Figures

Tables

Acknowledgements

Writing a book on a subject that is in constant flux has proved to be challenging but rewarding. Tax is a sensitive issue, and discussions in media show that people have strong opinions about it. In this book, we traced and analysed the development of the tax transparency phenomenon and its root causes. Our definition of tax transparency is based on companies' willingness to voluntarily provide tax-related information as part of their corporate social reporting initiatives. We aimed to balance theoretical discussion with empirical research and practical examples from companies that have been pioneering in tax transparency disclosures as early as 2012. Our intention has been to contribute to the understanding of the phenomenon, as well as advancing tax transparency in practice.

We would like to thank Professor of Taxation and Accounting Lynne Oats, University of Exeter Business School, for kindly agreeing to write a preface for our book. During the writing process, we received amazing support and feedback from tax researchers and experts that are too numerous to mention. Special thanks go to PhD Fellow Rasmus Corlin Christensen from Copenhagen Business School and Professor Martin Jacob from WHU Otto Beisheim School of Management.

Additionally, we would like to express our gratitude to participants at the Institute for Fiscal Studies residential conference 2016 Corporate Tax Avoidance: Where Next for Policy and Practice? with whom the book was discussed. The book idea also benefitted from discussants and participants' feedback received during the British Accounting and Finance Association conference in Bath in 2016.

We are grateful to the Global Reporting Initiative (GRI) for allowing us to use the text of the exposure draft of GRI topic-specific Standard on Tax and Payments to Governments and to the US Accountability Office for allowing us to use their figures of corporate taxes paid by US firms from 1950 to 2020.

Special thanks to Paul and Mark Middleton for their helpful feedback. We'd like to acknowledge Routledge for the excellent cooperation and supportive replies to our many enquiries.

During the years writing the book, we dedicated a lot of thought and part of our free time to the project. Therefore, we would especially like to thank our family members for their continuous understanding and support throughout the process.

Preface

Tax transparency is certainly a hot topic. The pressure to learn more about the tax affairs of multinationals has increased exponentially in recent years, albeit from a very low base. It was not so long ago that tax planning by multinationals was largely hidden from view, left to the exclusive purview of tax professionals and of negligible interest to outsiders, even academics. This book, therefore, is both timely and important.

The authors bring together a range of scholarship from both corporate social responsibility (CSR) and tax, both of which are fast-moving fields, and explore them in the context of tax disclosures by corporates. This is not a legal or technical book but is concerned more with disclosure *practices*, drawing on examples from a range of sources to demonstrate the mimetic isomorphism that is currently occurring as firms adapt to new social pressures for greater transparency. Tax information is losing its previously privileged status as confidential and, as the authors observe, we are now seeing a shift in the balance between the right to confidentiality and the right to know.

Publication of this book serves as a useful reminder that scholars of corporate disclosures have been thinking about the ways in which firms release information about their activities and affairs for some time, but for tax scholars, non-mandated disclosure of tax information is fairly new. The authors provide us with a brief overview of the differing perspectives from which researchers of CSR within business schools seek to understand corporate disclosure practices. They also develop a scale for measuring tax disclosures using both quantitative and qualitative data, which will provide inspiration for researchers for whom such modes of enquiry are meaningful.

Transparency is a complex phenomenon which can be viewed from many perspectives, providing scope for abundant misunderstandings. On the one hand, it can be a powerful tool for securing accountability. On the other, it can provide a mechanism for firms to hide information in plain sight, overloading regulatory bodies and confounding adjudicators. Most often, however, transparency is considered to be inherently beneficial and, therefore, worth pursuing. But assessing the costs and benefits of transparency initiatives is an empirical exercise. The authors of this volume assume the benefits outweigh the costs, as do most proponents of transparency, yet there is very little research verifying this. Indeed, many of the consequences of transparency, both negative and positive, are difficult to quantify.

Notwithstanding the lack of evidential backing for increasing demands for information, we are now moving down a path from which there may be no return. The need for more research into the fragile links between CSR and tax is, therefore, becoming more pressing, as excessive demands for disclosures may potentially give rise to aberrant responses from firms and in the end may be counterproductive.

We find both CSR and tax at the intersection of many academic disciplines. In the case of tax, each discipline tends to treat it as a peripheral, but also bounded, object of interest – largely examined without reference to research in other disciplines. The authors of this book demonstrate that tax scholars can learn from scholars in other fields, in this case CSR. Conversely, the book demonstrates that scholars of CSR can, and indeed should, take an interest in tax, particularly now that it has been brought into the open and out of the clutches of technical specialists.

Lynne Oats
Professor of Taxation and Accounting, Deputy Director,
Tax Administration Research Centre University
of Exeter, UK October 2019

Abbreviations

AEOI	Automatic Exchange of Information
AI	artificial intelligence
BEPS	base erosion and profit shifting
CbC	country-by-country
CCCTB	Common Consolidated Corporate Tax Base
CCO	corporate criminal offence
CDP	Carbon Disclosure Project
CFC	controlled foreign company
CIT	corporate income tax
CRD IV	Capital Requirements Directive IV
CSR	corporate social responsibility
CTS	corporate tax strategy
EC	European Commission
EITI	Extractive Industries Transparency Initiative
ESG	environmental, social, governance
ETR	effective tax rate
EU	European Union
FDI	foreign direct investment
GDPR	General Data Protection Regulation
GHG	greenhouse gas
GRI	Global Reporting Initiative
GSSB	Global Sustainability Standards Board
HMRC	Her Majesty's Revenue and Customs
ICIJ	International Consortium of Investigative Journalists
IFRS	International Financial Reporting Standards
IR	integrated reporting
ISA	International Standards on Auditing
ISRE	International Standard on Review Engagements
MNC	multinational corporation
MNE	multinational enterprise
NGO	non-governmental organisation
OECD	Organisation for Economic Co-operation and Development
PR	public relations

R&D	research and development
SASB	Sustainability Accounting Standards Board
SD	standard deviation
SEC	Securities and Exchange Commission
TCFD	Task Force on Climate-Related Financial Disclosures
TDI	tax disclosure index
UNSDGs	United Nations Sustainable Development Goals
UK	United Kingdom
US	United States
USA	United States of America
VAT	value-added tax
WTO	World Trade Organization

1 Overview of the corporate social responsibility (CSR) and tax landscape

Introduction

This chapter introduces the changing landscape of corporate social responsibility (CSR) and contextualises tax reporting as part of it. We address tax-related reforms worldwide that are meant to increase the transparency of the tax system. Chapter 1 provides regulators' views on the subject of tax reporting and disclosure by multinationals. This chapter is essential for placing our research in the rapidly changing world of tax-related international legislative forces. We provide examples of tax transparency reforms from the European Union (EU), countries falling into common law systems (USA, UK), code-law systems (Germany and France) and Finland. We explain the driving forces behind changing tax legislation for multinationals and highlight the difference between voluntary CSR reporting and instances when CSR and tax transparency are demanded by law. We provide examples of tax scandals, increased media attention and changing public opinion when citizens demand greater accountability and transparency from multinationals.

1.1 CSR landscape

1.1.1 Evolution of CSR

Voluntary reporting by companies on their environmental, social and economic performance going beyond legally required financial figures has become increasingly common, particularly since the 1990s. Such reporting is motivated by the CSR concept. According to the rationale behind CSR, companies need to consider their impacts on the environment and society going beyond the economic and financial realm. Additionally, they need to recognise the fact that they influence and are influenced by a large number of stakeholder groups. The proponents of CSR argue that companies' financial and CSR performance cannot be separated from each other in the modern world where various stakeholders increasingly emphasise CSR issues as opposed to simply focusing on financial figures. Financial performance and economic value creation are argued to be in many ways dependent on a company's success in operating sustainably regarding economic, social and environmental issues. This idea is referred to as the "triple bottom line" concept (Norman & MacDonald, 2004).

The EU defines CSR as "a concept whereby companies integrate social and environmental concerns in their business operations and in their interaction with stakeholders on a voluntary basis" (Hopkins, 2004, p. 6). Since its emergence in the 1970s, the concept has been described with many terms, including environmental accountability, responsibility policies, ethical policies, sustainability policies, corporate accountability, corporate social and environmental responsibility, etc. The CSR concept has been promoted by developments related to globalisation and increased awareness of and attention to companies' impacts on the environment and wider society. According to Adams (2004, p. 733), "The arguments for greater corporate accountability arise from the increases in size, power and global spread of multinational companies and increased awareness of the impacts of companies on the environment and local communities". The media, the Internet and the actions of non-governmental organisations (NGOs) have been instrumental in bringing about this global awareness.

Given the far-reaching global impact of multinational corporations (MNCs), it is logical that stakeholders interested in CSR issues target their demands particularly on that group of companies. In turn, the majority of multinationals have reacted to these demands and created varying policies, practices and reporting regarding sustainability issues. Consequently, our focus in this book is on the reporting of MNCs. A MNC is defined as "an enterprise that engages in foreign direct investment (FDI) and owns or, in some way, controls value-added activities in more than one country" (Dunning & Lundan, 2008, p. 3). The global scope of operation is highly relevant for our focus on tax transparency. The variance in tax rules between different national jurisdictions enables companies operating in several countries possibilities for differentiated tax strategies, resulting in different outcomes in tax expense.

The recent trend demonstrates that tax reporting is becoming an important part of CSR. Tax collected from MNEs has an impact on social, economic and environmental issues. For example, fair tax provides for social goods, promotes economic growth and covers environmental impacts, such as pollution in extractive industries, and contributes to local communities.

1.1.2 Legal enforcement of CSR reporting

Reporting their policies regarding environmental, social and economic responsibility issues and their performance in the sphere is one part of companies' CSR strategies. It is an important, but not the only, means of communicating about CSR. In 2017, 93% of the 250 largest companies in the world reported about their corporate responsibility activities (KPMG, 2017, p. 9). The reports carry various names – e.g. sustainability report, CSR report, responsibility report, citizenship report. Additionally, incorporating CSR information into annual reports and so-called integrated reporting (IR) has become increasingly common. We utilise the label "CSR reporting" to cover all reporting, including disclosure of issues falling under the definition of CSR.

Ideally, the production of CSR reports is motivated by the companies' desire to improve the sustainability of their operations, which would also be beneficial for long-term value creation and for decreasing business risks from non-financial sources (e.g. environmental accidents, labour abuse scandals, tax evasion accusations). In addition to conveying information to outside stakeholder groups, sustainability reporting helps companies to set goals, measure performance and manage change internally.

Critics of CSR see the reports as "greenwashing" (Hamann & Kapelus, 2004), by which companies seek to improve their image by claiming to take responsibility issues seriously but without taking any concrete actions. Such reporting amounts to a mere public relations strategy which has little material impact on actual sustainability performance. Since there is no global mandatory, official template for reporting, the practices and information included vary greatly between companies. Furthermore, the standards and stakeholder expectations differ between countries, which contributes to variations in CSR reporting internationally.

Several governments have taken national initiatives to advance CSR reporting either through legislation or recommendations. The 2016 Carrots & Sticks Survey identified in total 383 instruments in 64 different countries in Europe, Asia-Pacific, North America and Latin America (Bartels et al., 2016, p. 9). The initiatives vary in their focus, concerning only specific indicators – e.g. greenhouse gas (GHG) emissions – or specific industries – e.g. extractive industries or the financial sector. Additionally, the width of application differs, and reporting may be required only from listed companies. Additionally, some are mandatory and some voluntary: in the 2016 Carrots & Sticks Survey, 65% of the identified initiatives were classified as mandatory (Bartels et al., 2016, p. 12). It should be noted that financial accounting practice requires disclosures on all topics that may have material financial impact on the company. This covers, for example, environmental or social matters with significant consequences.

In France, the NRE Act 2001 (Nouvelles Régulations Économiques, New Economic Regulations) required that listed companies include environmental and social information in their annual reports. According to a 2007 governmental survey, 81% of companies had made some effort in terms of reporting although the law was a so-called orientation law without sanctions for non-compliance (Ministère des Affaires Etrangères – France, 2012). Subsequently, in 2012, the Grenelle Acts were implemented. The acts widened the breadth of companies required to report, broadened the amount of information required (although no specific mandatory indicators were defined), provided stricter rules on the quality of the report and required external verification (Ministère des Affaires Etrangères – France, 2012). Sweden demanded that all state-owned companies produce CSR reports in 2007 and to further the development, the government asked state-owned companies to set sustainability-related goals in 2012 and to report on them in 2014 (Swedish Institute, 2016). The German Sustainability Code was passed in 2011 by the German Council for Sustainable Development and endorsed by the federal government. The code provided companies with a voluntary instrument aimed at enhancing the transparency of companies' CSR performance (GRI, 2012). In the United Kingdom (UK), listed companies have been required to disclose information on human rights issues, gender representation in the company organisation and GHG emissions since 2013 on the basis of amendments to the Companies Act 2006 (GRI, 2013).

In Finland, the Finnish Accounting Act 1997 required large companies to include material non-financial information in the annual report and the Accounting Board issued guidelines for environmental disclosures in 2006. The Governmental Resolution on State Ownership Policy 2011 required certain state-owned companies to report their sustainability performance to encourage CSR reporting as good business practice more widely. The United States (US) has strict disclosure rules (most importantly, the Securities and Exchange Commission (SEC) regulations republished in 2008 and the Sarbanes-Oxley Act of 2002) that are applied to non-financial information as well. They require disclosure of all material information that may impact on investors' decision making regarding legislative compliance, judicial proceedings and liabilities relating to the environment, as well as governance matters. Additionally, there are several reporting instruments related to specific environmental or social topics (e.g. Business Supply Chain Transparency on Trafficking and Slavery Act 2015 and SEC Guidance on Disclosure Related to Climate Change, 2010).

As a step towards more unified reporting at the EU level, the EU adopted the directive on disclosure of non-financial and diversity information by certain large companies in December 2014 (Directive 2014/95/EU). The requirements apply from 2018 onwards to large public interest entities with more than 500 employees (approximately 6,000 companies). The directive covers information on a company's development, performance, position and the impact of its activities relating to (as a minimum) environmental, social and employees, respect for human rights, anti-corruption and bribery matters. The company needs to disclose its business model, policies, outcomes and risks regarding the matters listed, as well key performance indicators relevant to the particular business. The directive contains a so-called report or explain model, and hence companies do not need to report on all matters but are required to disclose reasons for not doing so. This directive, however, does not require any tax-related disclosure or country-by-country (CbC) tax reporting.

As the directive does not include any specific mandatory key CSR performance indicators, disclosures are likely to vary significantly amongst companies. In order to facilitate relevant, useful and comparable disclosure, the European Commission (EC) has produced non-binding guidelines on non-financial reporting (European Commission, 2017). Given that the guidelines specifically state that "the Commission encourages companies to avail themselves of the flexibility under the Directive when disclosing non-financial information" (European Commission, 2017), uniform reporting cannot be expected. The variation is in part necessary and appropriate, as different indicators are relevant to different entities due to their business models. Materiality is one of the key principles, meaning that assessment of material issues should be based on the thorough examination of the following factors: business model, strategy and principal risks; main sectoral issues; interests and expectations of relevant shareholders; impact of the activities; public policy and regulatory drivers. However, the directive also leaves space for variation in the extensiveness of reporting, and it can be expected that companies with more established or advanced CSR reporting practices report more extensively compared to those with little or no previous CSR disclosures.

1.1.3 CSR reporting standards

To improve the quality, credibility and comparability of companies' reports, some international initiatives for standardising the practice exist. Currently, the three most widely recognised CSR reporting standards are the GRI standards, AccountAbility's AA1000 Series and the United Nations (UN) Global Compact's Communication on Progress (Tschopp & Huefner, 2015). Additionally, the US-based Sustainability Accounting Standards Board (SASB) has worked since 2012 to develop industry-specific accounting principles for material sustainability topics. The most recent additions are the recommendations of Task Force on Climate-Related Financial Disclosures (TCFD), which aim to help companies disclose "clear, comparable and consistent information about the risks and opportunities presented by climate change" (TCFD, 2017, p. i), not only in CSR reports but also in public financial reporting. The variation in CSR reporting standards content determines that some standards emphasise more environmental reporting as opposed to social.

The GRI is the most popular reporting standard worldwide. GRI was established in 1997 offering a framework based on the "triple bottom line" concept: economic performance (economic impact on customers, suppliers, employees, capital providers and the public sector), social performance (indicators such as labour conditions and human rights) and environmental performance (indicators such as resource use, waste management and health risks). GRI scales the reports in accordance to its level of comprehensiveness (how many of the recommended issues are addressed in the report) and recommends external assurance to increase credibility. The GRI guidelines influence in CSR reporting has grown from only 44 companies following the framework in 2000 to 1,973 in 2010 (Ioannou & Serafeim, 2017, p. 2). At present, the GRI is the world's most widely used voluntary sustainability reporting framework. According to KPMG's International Survey of Corporate Responsibility Reporting, 80% of the 250 largest companies and 69% of the 100 largest companies in each country included in the survey adhere to GRI Sustainability Reporting Guidelines (KPMG, 2017, p. 28).

CSR frameworks and standards vary on whether tax is a part of CSR reporting and initiatives. In our assessment, we include GRI, AA1000, UN Global Compact, OECD Guidelines for MNCs, IR, SASB and TCFD reporting standards. The two remaining influential standards, CDP and GHG protocols, focus primarily on the environmental pillars; hence, they are not included in the analysis. Table 1.1 summarises the most prominent standards regarding their treatment of tax.

Table 1.1 demonstrates that of all CSR reporting standards, only GRI has an explicit indicator related to tax. While OECD for MNCs and IR consider tax issues relevant, there are no guidelines on the disclosure of tax issues. However, acknowledging the rising importance of tax matters as part of CSR, GRI published

Table 1.1 Tax as part of major CSR reporting standards

Reporting standard	*Focus*	*Inclusion of tax reporting*
GRI	Impacts on the environment, society and the economy	Disclosure 201-1 (previously indicator EC1) includes payments to governments by country Forthcoming topic-specific Standard on Tax and Payments to Governments
AA1000	Principles-based framework to prioritise, measure and respond to sustainability challenges inclusively and accountably	Not included
UN Global Compact	Do business responsibly by aligning their strategies and operations with ten principles on human rights, labour, environment and anti-corruption	Not included
OECD Guidelines for MNCs	Guidelines provide voluntary principles and standards for responsible business conduct consistent with applicable laws and internationally recognised standards	Corporate citizenship in the area of taxation implies that enterprises should comply with both the letter and the spirit of the tax laws and regulations in all countries in which they operate, co-operate with authorities and make information that is relevant or required by law available to them
IR	Promote a more cohesive and efficient approach to corporate reporting that draws on different reporting strands and communicates the full range of factors that materially affect the ability of an organisation to create value over time	An integrated report describes key outcomes, including the following: • Both internal outcomes (e.g. employee morale, organisational reputation, revenue and cash flows) and external outcomes (e.g. customer satisfaction, tax payments, brand loyalty and social and environmental effects) • Both positive outcomes (i.e. those that result in a net increase in the capitals and thereby create value) and negative outcomes (i.e. those that result in a net decrease in the capitals and thereby diminish value)
SASB	Enable companies to report financially material information on industry-specific sustainability topics most important to investors. Intended to be used in IR	Financial impacts in the form of consumption or environmental taxes (or tax credits) included
TCFD	Enable companies to disclose clear, comparable and consistent information about the risks and opportunities presented by climate change. Through that support the transparency and efficiency in the financial markets and the transition to a more sustainable, low-carbon economy	Tax matters are mentioned in relation to exposure to transition risks, as it is recognised that resource-intensive organisations with high GHG emissions may face additional taxes due to legislative changes aimed at curbing emissions

a draft standard Tax Payments to Governments in December 2018. This standard includes much more comprehensive guidelines for reporting on tax-related matters, including the governance and management of tax and tax risks, stakeholder engagement in relation to tax, tax strategy, corporate taxes paid and accrued by country and other taxes and payments to governments by country, as well as significant uncertain tax positions (GRI, 2018).

These CSR international frameworks and standards have been influential in determining the disclosures produced. Of the national initiatives, the German Sustainability Code is aligned with GRI. The EU Commission guidelines on non-financial reporting build on the existing reporting frameworks, including, for example, GRI, the International Integrated Reporting Framework, CDP, GSC (green supply chain), ISO 26000 and OECD Guidelines for Multinational Enterprises.

Although CSR reporting has been voluntary or subject to definitions of materiality in most jurisdictions, companies have made the extra effort and spent additional resources in order to produce CSR reports and offering disclosures exceeding the legally required minimum. The underlying motivations may relate to improving sustainability practices for producing savings, attracting capital from ethical investment funds, complying with borrowing requirements, industry-specific regulations or codes of conduct, enhancing company image and reputation, a genuine (altruistic) belief in an accountability to the surrounding society and satisfying different stakeholder groups' demands for information and accountability. We will examine the theories explaining the CSR phenomenon and tax transparency as a part of it in Chapter 3.

1.1.4 Tax as part of CSR

As opposed to the many mainly voluntary CSR activities, paying taxes is a legal obligation to companies and as such to an extent an unavoidable cost of doing business. As Williams (2007, p. 14) states, "Tax obligations are determined by statute law rather than by commercially agreed contracts". While companies are obliged to pay taxes by legislation, the practical implementation and amount of tax collected depend on companies' tax strategies. Thus, given the differences in tax rates globally, as well as tax exemptions and reliefs granted by governments, companies can pursue various strategies to minimise the taxes they incur. Tax planning can be used to increase efficiency of tax payments. Tax avoidance strategies are usually based on taking advantage of differing tax rates in different countries (including the use of tax havens[1]). Tools used include specific structuring of the company (e.g. establishing subsidiaries in foreign countries), transfer pricing, intra-corporation loans, etc. The possibilities for varied tax strategies have increased due to globalisation and can be most extensively used by MNCs whose operations and ownership are globally dispersed.

Tax is a financial transfer to the state, which uses the money to provide services to the public and hence guarantees the functioning of society.[2] Therefore, taxes can be seen as a contribution to social welfare. Refraining from aggressive tax-planning activities would result in a larger wealth transfer to the society, which constitutes socially responsible behaviour. Following this thinking, taxation has been incorporated into the CSR framework under the pillar of economic responsibility. That is the case in the GRI reporting framework: the guidelines' economic responsibility section includes an indicator "direct economic value created and distributed". Both the most recent GRI standards' disclosure 201–1 and previous versions of indicator EC1 include payments to governments by country.

The political economy framework offers an explanation as to why in different societies the issue of taxation as part of CSR is understood differently (Avi-Yonah, 2014). According to Avi-Yonah (2014), countries fall into liberal capitalism (USA, UK), corporatist societies (Germany) and statist societies (France). Countries with different varieties of capitalism view the company and, consequently, its responsibilities, including responsibility to pay taxes towards society, differently. Societies with liberal variety of capitalism (e.g. USA and UK) tend to have an aggregate or nexus-of-contracts view of the corporation, meaning that corporation is viewed merely as an aggregate of its individual members or shareholders. In this context, applying the CSR principles to taxation – i.e. not attempting to minimise taxes in all legal ways – would be an "illegitimate attempt by managers to tax shareholders without their consent, and lead to managers being unaccountable to the shareholders that elected them" (Avi-Yonah, 2014, p. 13). However, this would be self-defeating if taken to the extreme as it would follow that the state would be left without adequate resources to fulfil its governmental function and, consequently, the corporation would similarly be unable to fulfil its contractual responsibilities to society.

In corporatist societies (e.g. Germany and Japan), the dominant view of the corporation is the real entity view. There the corporation is viewed as an entity separate both from the State and its shareholders, having rights and obligations similar to an individual citizen. Following this, the corporation would not be required to engage in CSR actions going beyond that legal requirement, but it may be praised if it does so. Countries presenting the third variety of capitalism, the statist variety – e.g. France – display an artificial view of the corporation. According to this view, "The corporation owes its existence to the state and is granted certain privileges to be able to fulfill functions that the state would like to achieve" (Avi-Yonah, 2014, p. 12). This would imply that CSR functions are part of corporation's mission, and taxation could be viewed as one way of fulfilling CSR obligations.

In general, there are convincing arguments that paying a "fair" share of taxes is considered to be an integral part of responsible business. However, defining "fair" is a more contentious topic. The reasoning against strategic tax planning assumes that the state would use the funds raised more effectively for the benefit of the society than the company, but this assumption may not in all cases be entirely unproblematic. If the funds saved from the corporation's tax bill were used to develop the company's business – e.g. employ additional workers for research and development activities – this could just as well fulfil the criteria of using the funds effectively for the benefit of society. Indeed, critics argue that taxes in fact detract from social welfare since they damage innovation, production, job creation and economic development (Davis et al., 2016, p. 47). Furthermore, the company could, at least in theory, use the funds saved for some philanthropic purpose or other CSR aspect, which would contribute to the welfare of the society.

It is important to note that the success and continuance of companies' business activities is necessary for the functioning of the society (provision of goods and services, employment, tax income, etc.). It would be detrimental to society if companies' competitiveness was hampered by excessive tax burdens. Therefore, as Williams (2007) points out, voluntary payment of excessive tax liabilities could put a company at a competitive disadvantage, which places other stakeholders, such as employees and investors, at risk. Therefore, paying excessive taxes to the extent that it harms the business does not seem to be socially responsible behaviour. Furthermore, states often put incentives in tax systems (e.g. tax reliefs for R&D activities) designed to promote certain behaviour with the intention that companies take advantage of them. In these cases, using tax planning to take advantage of these incentives specifically put in place by the state would not seem socially irresponsible. In sum, there is no single guideline on how CSR principles can be used to establish the "fair" amount of tax (above the legally required minimum) that the company should pay in order to be socially responsible.

To discover companies' stance on taxation as part of CSR, the connection between companies' CSR activities and their tax policy has been empirically researched. The findings are not fully consistent regarding whether companies view paying taxes as socially responsible behaviour. Based on their research on US companies, Davis et al. (2016, p. 31) conclude that "on average, managers and other stakeholders do not view the payment of corporate taxes as an important part of a public corporation's socially responsible behavior". Their conclusion is based on the negative relation Davis et al. (2016) found between the level of CSR and the effective tax rate company reports. However, Lanis and Richardson (2012, p. 86) found the opposite phenomenon among Australian companies: "The higher the level of CSR disclosure of a corporation, the lower is the level of corporate tax aggressiveness". More recent research from Lanis and Richardson (2015, p. 439) employing US data from 2003–2009 indicate that "more socially responsible firms are likely to display less tax avoidance". Watson's (2015) research on US companies incorporates the impact of resource scarcity. He finds that "a lack of social responsibility is positively associated with tax avoidance in firms with low current or future earnings performance, but this effect is diminished when current or future earnings performance is high" (Watson, 2015, p. 19). Furthermore, "social responsibility is positively associated with tax avoidance when current earnings performance low but not when it is high" (2015, p. 19). This suggests that poor earnings performance– i.e. scarce resources – prevents responsible companies from applying their commitment to CSR to their tax policy. In the absence of this restraint, the more socially responsible companies seem to apply more socially responsible tax strategies.

The results are not fully comparable, as they use different proxies for the level of CSR performance and tax aggressiveness. Furthermore, most of the research has used data on American companies (except for Lanis & Richardson, 2012). Given that it is reasonable to expect that views and attitudes towards taxation may vary across countries due to the varieties of capitalism (following, for example, Avi-Yonah, 2014) and consequent societal norms, the results should not be generalised too hastily.

The analysis of CSR reporting standards demonstrates that GRI, OECD for MNCs, IR and TCFD include some tax-related guidelines with variation in disclosure extensiveness. It is important to emphasise that, in discussing tax transparency in CSR context, we do not address the debate on the moral responsibilities of the corporation nor tax avoidance schemes. By analysing the theoretical background of tax reporting in CSR context, we would like to see how transparent an enterprise wants to be in its tax activities by voluntarily disclosing information on its tax activities.

1.2 Tax regulation reforms worldwide

Companies are required to disclose basic corporate income tax figures as part of their standard financial reporting. However, as a reaction to companies' tax avoidance policies, legislative requirements and voluntary initiatives that establish more extensive and transparent disclosure requirements emerged in the 2000s.

The taxation of multinational companies is a challenging and complex issue. Forstater and Christensen (2017) provide an overview of how in recent years, tax issues of multinationals have shifted from technical discussion to the public and political domains. They argue that seven key groups play roles in shaping the current tax debate: Tax Justice Network, development NGOs, transparency and accountability NGOs, international bureaucracies (OECD, EC), media, political champions and funder foundations (see Figure 1.1). Tax debate players vary in their tax-specific expertise and resource capacity. For instance, the Tax Justice Network, while possessing high tax-specific expertise, has very low resources capacity, while the media has both low tax-specific expertise and low resource capacity but at the same time has a huge impact in attracting public attention to tax scandals. Funder foundations represented by – e.g. the Transparency and Accountability Initiative and Norway – have been influential in promoting increased tax transparency and CbC reporting. Funder foundations are placed in the low expertise and high resource quadrant since they enabled the popularisation and politicisation of international tax debate without a direct focus on the technical tax issues.

Figure 1.1 demonstrates that the most prominent and influencing group falls under the category of international bureaucracies, represented by, for example, OECD and EC, which possess both high resource capacity and tax expertise. In our review of changing tax landscape, we concentrate on the initiatives promoted by international bureaucracies OECD and EC, because they have both tax-specific expertise and resource capacity to implement their regulative initiatives.

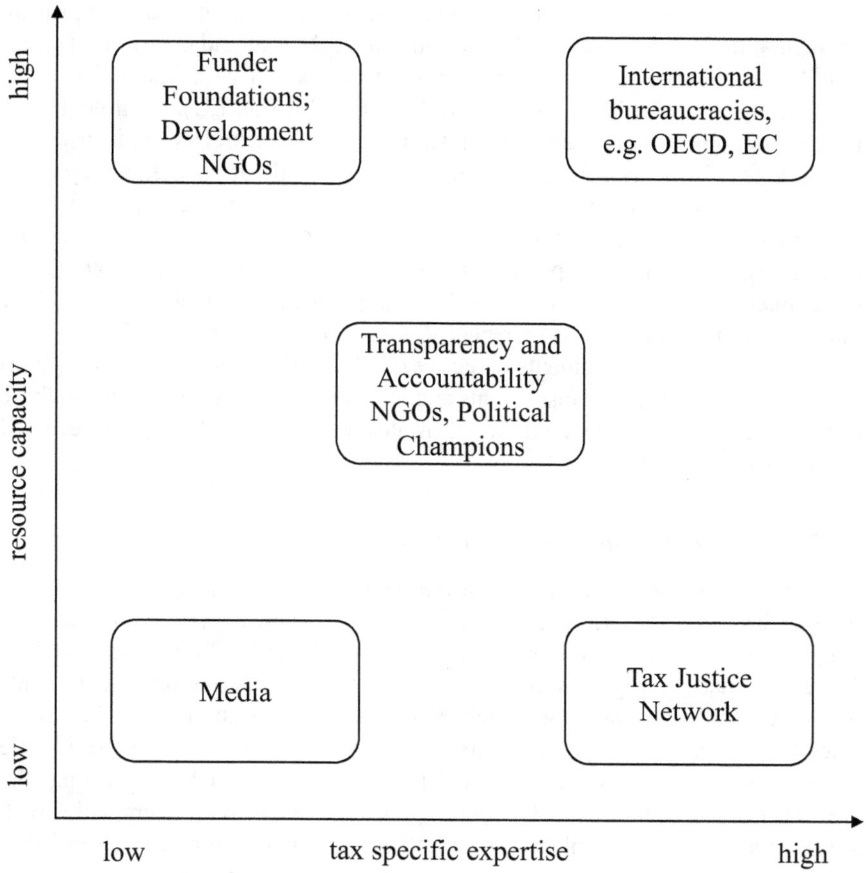

Figure 1.1 Key groups shaping tax debate

Source: Adopted from Forstater & Christensen (2017)

We also discuss an early initiative of corporate and government fiscal transparency, Extractive Industries Transparency Initiative (EITI).

1.2.1 Industry-specific tax transparency initiatives

First, tax transparency initiatives targeted specific sectors – namely, extractive industries (oil, gas, minerals, logging) or credit institutions and investment companies. The EITI standard was launched in 2002 after active civil society campaigning by the 'Publish What You Pay Coalition' of over 800 NGOs (Forstater & Christensen, 2017, p. 13). In 2017, EITI was implemented by 52 resource-rich countries. It requires companies in the extractive sector to publish what they have paid to the governments in the countries implementing the standard and for the governments to disclose what they have received. In addition to taxes, this includes entitlements, royalties, dividends, bonuses, fees and other significant payments. In the US, the Dodd-Frank Wall Street Reform and Consumer Protection Act established similar requirements for the extractive industries. The EU Accounting Directive 2013, Chapter 10 (Directive 2013/34/EU), required the EU public-listed entities and large EU undertakings in the extractive industries and the logging of primary forests to publicly report details of payments they make to governments on an annual and per-country basis, including at project level. This includes disclosure of taxes paid, production rights, royalties, bonuses and other transactions made on payments of €100,000 and over. Each EU countries' government makes sure that the directive is implemented in national law, and the majority of the companies were expected to start reporting from 2017.

The EU Capital Requirements Directive (CRD IV, Directive 2013/36/EU) from June 2013 targeted credits institutions and investment companies, requiring these to report activities, turnover, number of employees, profit, public support received and taxes by country.

1.2.2 OECD base erosion and profit shifting

The most influential and extensive development targeted at increasing tax transparency has been the OECD base erosion and profit shifting (BEPS) action plan adopted by the OECD and G20 countries in 2013. The BEPS package provides 15 actions that equip governments with domestic and international instruments needed to tackle tax-planning strategies that exploit gaps and mismatches in tax rules to artificially shift profits to low- or no-tax locations where there is little or no economic activity (OECD, 2017). Specifically related to reporting, the BEPS action 13 includes a CbC reporting package that provides companies with a guideline to report annually their tax-related information for each tax jurisdiction in which they do business (revenues, profits, taxes paid and certain measures of economic activity). The reporting has become legally binding as countries have incorporated the requirements into their legislation since 2016. Additionally, the action 13 includes a framework, which sets out conditions and operational aspects for the exchange of CbC reports under the multilateral convention on mutual administrative assistance in tax matters. Tax information is reported to tax jurisdictions, and hence there is no requirement to produce any publicly available report. This means that multinational companies have had CbC tax information readily available since 2016 for publishing in CSR reporting, if they so choose.

1.2.3 EC tax transparency initiatives

The EC initiated a tax transparency package in 2015. The package includes actions to combat tax evasion, fraud and avoidance that are practised by MNCs. A concrete example of tax transparency measures is the Anti-Tax Avoidance

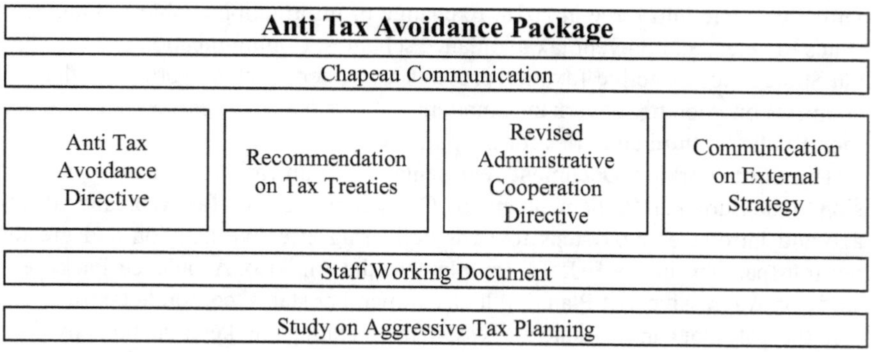

Figure 1.2 EC Anti-Tax Avoidance Package
Source: EC

Package (see Figure 1.2), which contains several elements to prevent aggressive tax planning and boost tax transparency and create a level playing field for all businesses in the EU. Chapeau Communication provides an overview of the political, economic and international context of the Anti-Tax Avoidance Package and its elements.

The Anti-Tax Avoidance Directive (Council Directive (EU) 2016/1164), as part of the Anti-Tax Avoidance Package, was adopted in 2016. It contains five legally binding anti-abuse measures:

- Controlled foreign company (CFC) rule to deter profit shifting to a low-/no-tax country
- Switchover rule to prevent double non-taxation of certain income
- Exit taxation to prevent companies from avoiding tax when re-locating assets
- Interest limitation to discourage artificial debt arrangements designed to minimise taxes
- General anti-abuse rule: to counteract aggressive tax planning when other rules do not apply

All member states must apply these measures from 1 January 2019 onwards.

Recommendation on Tax Treaties provides advice on how member states can reinforce their tax treaties against abuse by aggressive tax planners in an EU-law compliant way. A separate study on aggressive tax planning investigates member states' corporate tax rules (or lack thereof) that can facilitate aggressive tax planning. Aggressive tax-planning evaluations are also incorporated in the staff working document.

The Revised Administrative Cooperation Directive has as its objective CbC reporting between member states' tax authorities on key tax-related information on multinationals operating in the EU. The revised Administrative Cooperation Directive came into force in 2018. Exchange of information enables all member states to detect and prevent tax avoidance schemes. Communication on an External Strategy for Effective Taxation presents an EU approach to working with third countries on good tax governance matters and sets out a process to create a common EU list of third countries for tax purposes.

The Staff Working Document represents Communication from the Commission to the European Parliament and the Council on the Anti-Tax Avoidance Package and introduces next steps towards delivering effective taxation and greater tax transparency in the EU. To complement the Anti-Tax Avoidance Package a study on Aggressive Tax Planning looks at member states' corporate tax rules (or lack thereof) that can facilitate aggressive tax planning and key structures used by companies to avoid taxation. It provides factsheets with the main findings for each member state and examples of tactics used by multinationals to lower their taxes.

In addition to the Anti-Tax Avoidance Package of 2016, the EU has relaunched the Common Consolidated Corporate Tax Base (CCCTB), which stands for is a single set of rules to calculate companies' taxable profits in the EU. The CCCTB will be implemented through a two-step process and will be mandatory for the largest groups in the EU. A new set of rules will allow cross-border companies to comply with one single EU system for computing their taxable income, rather than many different national rulebooks.

The increase of tax transparency is designed so that intermediaries, such as tax advisors, accountants and lawyers who design tax schemes, become liable to report to the tax authorities on the schemes that qualify as aggressive tax arrangements. Compulsory reporting by intermediaries that may be providing services qualifying as aggressive tax planning was enforced from May 2018 by a Directive on the mandatory disclosure and exchange of cross-border tax arrangements (Council Directive (EU) 2018/822).

The EC has in 2016 proposed to extend the public CbC reporting requirement included the Accounting Directive 2013/34/EU Chapter 10 for the extractive and logging industries to cover all multinational groups with net consolidated turnover of at least €750 million. The proposal's reporting requirements include income tax accrued and paid as well as profit, turnover, accumulated earnings and employee numbers per country (European Commission, 2016).

1.2.4 National-level tax transparency reforms

Apart from the global and EU-based initiatives, several countries have implemented national rules to advance tax-related disclosures.

Tax reporting by state-owned companies in Finland

Since 2015, Finnish companies with majority state ownership have been required to publish quantitative and qualitative information regarding taxation. The directive was issued in order to achieve greater transparency in the spirit of the OECD BEPS action plan. Reporting must include taxes paid (as well as revenue, profit or number of personnel to facilitate comparability) divided by tax type on a CbC basis as well as tax strategy and principles. Additionally, taxes paid to and collected for states defined as tax havens by the OECD and any support received from them must be reported. The directive allows companies to determine the materiality of information, the appropriate reporting level regarding tax types and the format of reporting (VNK, 2014).

German initiatives

In 2017, German legislators introduced a law on combatting tax avoidance and amended further tax legislation which aimed to address tax evasion by imposing increased transparency requirements. Furthermore, in 2017, the German Ministry of Finance published final rules on German transfer pricing documentation. These changes in legislation are in line with the OECD BEPS project (Reggelin, 2017).

UK Finance Act 2016

The UK government introduced significant tax disclosure requirements in December 2016. The Finance Act 2016 made it compulsory for over 2,000 large companies to publish their tax strategy online (Deloitte, 2018). More specifically, companies need to state their approach to tax risk management and governance, attitude towards tax planning, the level of tax risk the company is prepared to accept and the approach to dealings with Her Majesty's Revenue and Customs (HMRC), all in relation to and so far as affecting UK taxation. The tax strategy may include other information related to UK or overseas taxation (Finance Act 2016). The act entered into force 15 December 2016 and applies to financial periods starting on or after that date. Although the requirement is not connected to any CSR framework, but is part of UK tax legislation, some companies refer to the mandatory tax strategy report in their separate CSR disclosures. We will look at some examples of these tax strategy reports in later chapters.

UK Sanctions and Anti-Money Laundering Act 2018

Amendments to the Sanctions and Anti-Money Laundering Act 2018 forces 14 British overseas territories to create public registers of beneficial ownership by 2020 or have the UK government impose them. British overseas territories, such as Bermuda, British Virgin Islands and Cayman Islands, are included in the EU blacklist of tax havens. The amendment to the Sanctions and Anti-Money Laundering Act 2018 is believed to make it easier to uncover corruption, tax evasion and tax avoidance.

1.2.5 EU blacklist of tax havens

The EU announced a blacklist of tax havens in December 2017. In total, 17 countries were named as "non-cooperative jurisdictions" (including small island states, such as Panama, United Arab Emirates, Republic of Korea, Namibia and Tunisia) with a further 47 put on notice. Several non-EU countries were screened and assessed against criteria for good governance, including tax transparency, fair taxation, implementation of OECD BEPS measures (European Council, 2017). The countries listed are encouraged to address the identified shortcomings in order to be removed from list and the development is monitored by the EU. However, no EU-level sanctions were implemented. The process and the resulting list have been criticised for not including any EU member states and omitting certain major offshore hubs – for example, the British Overseas Territories Bermuda, British Virgin Islands and Cayman Islands (ICIJ, 2017).

The contributing factor to polarised debate and even more engaging civic society in the tax reporting by multinationals was the leak of tax havens data intermediated by the International Consortium of Investigative Journalists (ICIJ). The most cited are Mossack Fonnseca ("Panama Papers") and "Paradise Papers". The "Panama Papers", revealed in 2015, contain an unprecedented amount of information, including more than 11 million documents covering 210,000 companies in 21 offshore jurisdictions. Each transaction spans across a number of different jurisdictions and may involve multiple entities and individuals. The "Paradise Papers", leaked in 2017, contain a set of 13.4 million confidential electronic documents relating to offshore investments. These documents fuelled discussion on the ethical aspect of tax avoidance by multinationals and contributed to stricter rules for tax reporting (by multinationals). These tax scandals are our focus in the next section.

1.3 Tax scandals and changing public opinion

The emergence of tax reporting requirements described in the previous section can be better understood when examining the developments brought by globalisation in the past decades and increased public attention to tax matters. Globalisation has given rise to numerous global MNCs and whose budgets exceed those of smaller countries. Companies and consulting professionals have become skilled in using different tax laws between countries to their advantage constructing corporate structures in a way that optimises or minimises their tax burden. The impact of corporate taxation on local economies is significant given the magnitude of financial flows that MNCs generate and transfer between countries. According to OECD (2015), "Research undertaken since 2013 confirms the potential magnitude of the BEPS problem, with estimates indicating annual losses of anywhere from 4–10% of global corporate income tax (CIT) revenues, i.e. USD 100 to 240 billion annually". In developing countries, the impact is even starker as their economies rely more heavily on corporate tax as a source of revenue.

The issue started as a technical debate amongst experts in the 1960s but has in the 20th century become a topic of interest to the wide public due to increased media attention. In the 1960s and 1970s, academics produced research on the issue of corporate tax avoidance, highlighting how international tax rules were outdated in the globalising world. Additionally, civil society organisations raised national tax justice campaigns in the UK and USA. However, these initiatives did not raise significant media attention or debate and consequently had little impact. The first NGO to research the tax issue in-depth from an international perspective was Oxfam, and its seminal report on tax havens was published in 2000. In 2003, one of the advisors involved in the project, John Christensen, went on to found the Tax Justice Network, an NGO that specialises in international tax issues (Forstater & Christensen, 2017).

The global financial crisis starting in 2008 can be seen as a turning point in the tax debate. As national governments saw their revenue declining, the issue of tax avoidance by corporations moved up the political agenda. In 2009, G20 leaders agreed on measures aimed at ending the era of bank secrecy, compelling countries considered tax havens to sign bilateral treaties that enabled the exchange of bank information. These declarations gained media attention, which in turn brought the issue to the general public's awareness. Additionally, development NGOs, such as Oxfam, Christian Aid and Action Aid tied tax issues to their established issue agendas – i.e. poverty and development (Forstater & Christensen, 2017). Investigative journalism focused on large and well-known corporations and in-depth reports of their aggressive tax planning strategies featured in mainstream media. For example, Dowling (2014, p. 177) notes that "[i]n 2011–2012 high-profile companies like Amazon, Apple, Bank of America, Boeing, Cadbury, Chevron, eBay, Exxon Mobil, Google, IKEA, Microsoft, News Corporation, Hewlett-Packard, and Starbucks have all received bad publicity about their tax practices", adding that General Electric (GE) had been singled out as "the Poster Child of US tax avoidance practice". A *New York Times* article by Kocieniewski (2011) highlighted the wide variety of legal tax avoidance schemes that enabled GE to avoid paying any tax in the US during 2009–2010 despite making 14.2 billion USD profit worldwide, of which 5.1 billion USD was in the US.

In the UK, Reuters published Tom Bergin's special report on Starbucks' tax avoidance in 2012. Bergin (2012) reported that the UK subsidiary's profits were nulled through royalty and intra-group loan arrangements with the result that the company had paid no corporation tax in Britain since 2009, although it communicated to investors that its UK operations were profitable. Similar criticism on tax avoidance by means of artificial arrangements exploiting national differences in corporate tax rates across Europe was raised against other large multinationals – namely, Apple, Google, Facebook and Amazon. Following general public disapproval, the UK parliament acted and the executives of Starbucks, as well as Google and Amazon, were called to parliamentary hearings on tax avoidance in 2012. In response to the public criticism, Starbucks, for instance, declared in 2014 that it would move its European offices to London, which would result in larger tax payments in the UK (Jolly, 2014).

A professional services company EY (2013, p. 16) summarises how widespread media coverage of taxation-related matters was already in 2013:

> During the first week of April this year, articles on tax avoidance appeared in the national press of, amongst others, Egypt, India, New Zealand, Pakistan, South Korea, Spain, Taiwan, the UK and the US. The media in many of the same countries covered tax havens as did newspapers in Australia, Belgium, France, Germany, Malaysia and the Netherlands.

The individual cases have inarguably gained significant attention, but the large-scale leaks of confidential information from tax havens, such as 2014 "Lux Leaks", 2016 "Panama Papers" and 2017 "Paradise Papers", dominated headlines and were met by public outcry when published. Indeed, the 2000s have thus far witnessed several leaks of secret files that contain information on wealthy individuals' and companies' financial arrangements and related taxation activities. The investigations have been led by the ICIJ, a global non-profit network of journalists from several countries who collaborate on in-depth investigative stories. The ICIJ received the material from different sources. Although the companies and individuals being mentioned in the leaked papers have inarguably gained negative publicity, in most cases, their actions have not been illegal.

The series began in 2013 with Offshore Leaks that revealed the names of more than 120,000 companies and trusts in different tax havens. These companies and trusts were tied to a mix of politicians, government officials and their families in Russia, China, Azerbaijan, Canada, Thailand, Mongolia, Pakistan and the Philippines (BBC, 2017a). The Luxemburg Leaks published in the following year contained material leaked from the professional services firm PricewaterhouseCoopers (PwC) in Luxembourg. It revealed how over 340 companies had taken advantage of the favourable tax rulings in Luxembourg between 2002 and 2010. ICIJ's list included well-known companies, such as FedEx, Pepsi, Amazon and IKEA (ICIJ, 2014a; ICIJ, 2014b; The Guardian, 2014; Süddeutsche Zeitung, 2014). The first set of materials was followed by another leak of confidential documents obtained from other "Big 4" accounting firms and published in December 2014. This leak expanded the list of companies involved in tax deals in Luxembourg with names such as the Walt Disney Co., Koch Industries Inc. and 33 other companies (ICIJ, 2014b).

The ICIJ investigation, known as the Swiss Leaks, focusing on the HSBC Private Bank (Suisse) was published in February 2015. It was significant in the sense that it uncovered information from Switzerland, the country known for its strong banking secrecy. ICIJ (2015) argued that the leaked documents revealed how the subsidiary of HSBC had "continued to offer services to clients who had been unfavourably named by the United Nations, in court documents and in the media as connected to arms trafficking, blood diamonds and bribery" as well as to those connected with discredited regime. The ICIJ also argued that the materials showed how the bank's employees had discussed with clients "a range of measures that would ultimately allow clients to avoid paying taxes in their home countries" and assured non-disclosure of account details to national authorities (ICIJ, 2015). The clients who held HSBC bank accounts included politicians from Britain, Russia, Ukraine, Georgia, Romania, India, Liechtenstein, Mexico, Lebanon, Tunisia and several other African states (ICIJ, 2015).

The largest leak by far in terms of the amount of material was the "Panama Papers" published by ICIJ and its partners in April 2016. BBC (2017a) reports that the confidential files from a Panamanian law firm Mossack Fonseca were given to a German newspaper Süddeutsche Zeitung by an anonymous source. The revelations contained information on the offshore investments of over 120 prominent individuals (politicians, celebrities, billionaires), resulting, for example, in the resignation of the prime minister of Iceland and the dismissal of the prime minister in Pakistan (BBC, 2017a). ICIJ (2016) reported that the the law firm had operated with most of the important international banks in order to enable their clients to take advantage of the tax-haven system (BBC, 2017a). The leak dominated news headlines at the time and the public outcry was significant. Consequently, governments took legislative action to curb the tax loopholes enabling legal tax avoidance that was, however, viewed as unethical by the media and public.

The most recent leak in November 2017, titled the "Paradise Papers", was similarly published by the ICIJ after the German newspaper Süddeutsche Zeitung obtained the documents. The main company involved was Appleby, the headquarters of which are located in Bermuda, but the documents feature several other offshore jurisdictions as well. The revelations involved the financial arrangements of numerous wealthy politicians and celebrities, as well as multinational companies, including Apple, Facebook, Nike, Siemens, Allianz and Deutsch Bank (Focus DE, 2017; BBC, 2017b).

Figure 1.3 presents a timeline of the major tax cases in the media and tax legislation initiatives mentioned in this chapter.

Media attention has raised the matter in public consciousness: research by the Pew Research Center and the Institute of Business Ethics show that tax avoidance is one of the prime concerns that the general public in the US and UK has about the tax system and companies' behaviour. Research conducted by the Pew Research Center (2017) in the US discovered that the main frustration Americans have with the federal tax system is that some corporations do not pay their fair share (62 % of respondents answered that this bothers them "a lot"). Institute of Business Ethics's (2017, p. 3) surveys on the attitudes of the British public to business ethics conducted in 2012–2016 illustrate how corporate tax avoidance has risen up the agenda. In response to the question about which company behaviour most needs addressing, corporate tax avoidance has been the most popular answer since 2013.

	Tax regulation	Tax revelations in the media	
2008			2008
2009	G20 "end of the era of bank secrecy"	Guardian "The Tax Gap" series	2009
2010	US Dodd-Frank Act		**2010**
2011		NY Times G.E. coverage	2011
2012		UK Reuters Starbucks UK parliamentary hearings (Starbucks, Google, Apple)	2012
2013	OECD BEPS EU Accounting Directive, EU CRD IV	Offshore leaks	2013
2014		Luxemburg Leaks	2014
2015	EU tax transparency package and CCCTB initiated	Swiss Leaks	**2015**
2016	EU Anti Tax Avoidance Directive OECD CbC reporting requirement implemented	Panama Papers Bahamas Papers	2016
2017	EU black list of tax havens	Paradise Papers	2017
2018	EU Directive on the mandatory disclosure and exchange of cross-border tax arrangements (DAC6)		2018
2019			2019
2020			**2020**

Figure 1.3 Timeline of tax cases in the media and tax legislation initiatives

Following this development in public attitudes, the impact of tax strategies on corporate image has become a more important issue on the corporate executives' agenda. In EY's 2017 tax risk and controversy survey, "[m]ore than half (55%) of all survey respondents said that tax controversy management has become somewhat or significantly more important for their business in the past two years", and for larger businesses, the figure is even higher at 64% (EY, 2017).

Summary

Tax transparency has received increased attention in recent years, mainly due to the revelation by the media of tax scandals, tax evasion and tax avoidance cases by multinationals. Analysis of legislative landscape in the tax domain reveals that OECD and EC are shaping the scene by introducing comprehensive set of tax transparency issues. Individual countries – e.g. Germany and the UK – have introduced their own legislations to improve tax transparency. We observe a mirroring phenomenon whereby major tax scandals correspond with the legislative initiatives, and in some instances create a momentum to speed the implementation of tax avoidance reforms.

By posing the question if tax is viewed as part of companies' CSR strategy, we analysed current CSR frameworks and standards. Tax disclosures are included in

OECD for MNE, GRI and IR standards. However, the voluntary nature of CSR standards and companies' own reporting motives leaves significant space for variation between countries and companies on whether extensive tax disclosures are part of socially responsible behaviours. Multinationals prepare tax transparency data that governments increasingly require from them, but are they ready to disclose it to a greater public as part of their CSR initiatives? We address this question in Chapter 3, looking at the underlying theories why multinationals may choose to be tax transparent to a larger set of stakeholders in their CSR disclosures.

Notes

1 OECD has defined four key factors that identify a territory as a tax haven: (1) no or only nominal taxes, (2) lack of effective exchange of information, (3) lack of transparency and (4) no substantial corporate activities required (Preuss, 2010, p. 367).
2 State is seen here as a surrogate for society, following Williams (2007, p. 12).

References

Adams, C. A., 2004, 'The Ethical, Social and Environmental Reporting-Performance Portrayal Gap', *Accounting, Auditing & Accountability Journal*, 17 (5), pp. 731–757.

Avi-Yonah, R. S., 2014, 'Corporate Taxation and Corporate Social Responsibility', *New York University Journal of Law & Business*, 11 (1), pp. 1–29.

Bartels, W., Fogelberg, T., Hoballah, A. and van der Lugt, C., 2016, 'Carrots & Sticks: Global Trends in Sustainability Reporting Regulation and Policy', Available at www.carrotsandsticks.net/wp-content/uploads/2016/05/Carrots-Sticks-2016.pdf. Accessed 07/08/2018.

BBC, 2017a, 'Paradise Papers: Your Guide to Four Years of Offshore Revelations', Available at www.bbc.com/news/business-41877932. Accessed 30/12/2017.

BBC, 2017b, 'Paradise Papers: Everything You Need to Know about the Leak', Available at www.bbc.com/news/world-41880153. Accessed 30/12/2017.

Bergin, T., 2012, 'Special Report: How Starbucks Avoids UK Taxes', *Reuters*. Available at https://uk.reuters.com/article/uk-britain-starbucks-tax/special-report-how-starbucks-avoids-uk-taxes-idUKBRE89E0EW20121015. Accessed 30/12/2017.

Davis, A. K., Guenther, D. A., Krull, L. K. and Williams, B. M., 2016, 'Do Socially Responsible Firms Pay More Taxes?', *The Accounting Review*, 91 (1), pp. 47–68.

Deloitte, 2018, 'Tax Strategies in the Spotlight', Available at www2.deloitte.com/uk/en/pages/tax/articles/tax-transparency.html. Accessed 07/08/2018.

Dowling, G. R., 2014, 'The Curious Case of Corporate Tax Avoidance: Is It Socially Irresponsible?', *Journal of Business Ethics*, 124, pp. 172–184.

Dunning, J. H. and Lundan, S. M., 2008, *Multinational enterprises and the global economy* (2nd ed.), Cheltenham, Edward Elgar Publishing.

European Commission, 2015, 'Tax Transparency Package', *EC Publications*. Available at https://ec.europa.eu/taxation_customs/business/company-tax/tax-transparency-package_en#heading_5. Accessed 17/10/2018.

European Commission, 2016, 'Proposal for a Directive of the European Parliament and of the Council Amending Directive 2013/34/EU as Regards Disclosure of Income Tax

Information by Certain Undertakings and Branches', *2016/0107 (COD)*. Available at https://eur-lex.europa.eu/legal-content/EN/TXT/PDF/?uri=CELEX:52016PC0198&from=EN. Accessed 31/07/2019.

European Commission, 2017, 'Communication from the Commission: Guidelines on Non-Financial Reporting (Methodology for Reporting Non-Financial Information)', *2017/C 215/01*. Available at https://eur-lex.europa.eu/legal-content/EN/TXT/?uri=OJ%3AC%3A2017%3A215%3ATOC. Accessed 08/06/2019.

European Council, 2017, 'Common EU List of Third Country Jurisdictions for Tax Purposes', Available at https://ec.europa.eu/taxation_customs/tax-common-eu-list_en. Accessed 30/12/2017.

EY, 2013, 'Tax Transparency: Seizing the Initiative', Available at www.ey.com/Publication/vwLUAssets/Tax_Transparency_-_Seizing_the_initiative/$FILE/EY_Tax_Transparency.pdf. Accessed 30/12/2017.

EY, 2017, 'EY's 2017 Tax Risk and Controversy Survey Series', Available at www.ey.com/gl/en/services/tax/ey-dimming-the-glare-trends-in-tax-controversy. Accessed 30/12/2017.

Focus DE, 2017, 'Paradise Papers: Neue Enthüllungen zu Steuer-Tricks bringen Politiker unter Druck', Available at www.focus.de/finanzen/steuern/paradise-papers-neue-enthuellungen-zu-steuer-tricks-bringen-politiker-unter-druck_id_7805051.html. Accessed 30/12/2017.

Forstater, M. and Christensen, R. C., 2017, 'New Players, New Game: The Role of the Public and Political Debate in the Development of Action on International Tax Issues', *European Tax Policy Forum*. Available at http://etpf.org/resphase12.html. Accessed 17/10/2018.

GRI, 2012, 'Focus on Germany: The Uptake of Sustainability Disclosure Measures by Europe's Largest Economy', Available at www.globalreporting.org/information/news-and-press-center/Pages/Focus-on-Germany-the-uptake-of-sustainability-disclosure-measures-by-Europes-largest-economy.aspx. Accessed 30/12/2017.

GRI, 2013, 'New Reforms Strengthen Non-Financial Reporting in the UK', Available at www.globalreporting.org/information/news-and-press-center/Pages/New-reforms-strengthen-non-financial-reporting-in-the-UK-.aspx. Accessed 30/12/2017.

GRI, 2018, 'Disclosures on Tax and Payments to Government', *Project Page*. Available at www.globalreporting.org/standards/work-program-and-standards-review/disclosures-on-tax-and-payments-to-government. Accessed 08/06/2019.

The Guardian, 2014, 'Luxembourg Tax Files: How Tiny State Rubber-Stamped Tax Avoidance on an Industrial Scale', Available at www.theguardian.com/business/2014/nov/05/-sp-luxembourg-tax-files-tax-avoidance-industrial-scale. Accessed 30/12/2017.

Hamann, R. and Kapelus, P., 2004, 'Corporate Social Responsibility in Mining in Southern Africa: Fair Accountability or Just Greenwash?', *Development*, 47 (3), pp. 85–92.

Hopkins, M., 2004, *Corporate social responsibility: An issues paper*. Working Paper No. 27, Policy Integration Department, Commission on the Social Dimension of Globalization, International Labour Office, Geneva.

ICIJ, 2014a, 'Leaked Documents Expose Global Companies' Secret Tax Deals in Luxembourg', Available at www.icij.org/investigations/luxembourg-leaks/leaked-documents-expose-global-companies-secret-tax-deals-luxembourg/. Accessed 22/07/2019.

ICIJ, 2014b, 'New Leak Reveals Luxembourg Tax Deals for Disney, Koch Brothers Empire', Available at www.icij.org/investigations/luxembourg-leaks/new-leak-reveals-luxembourg-tax-deals-disney-koch-brothers-empire/. Accessed 30/12/2017.

ICIJ, 2015, 'ICIJ Website, Section on Swiss Leaks', Available at www.icij.org/investigations/swiss-leaks/. Accessed 30/12/2017.

ICIJ, 2016, 'A new ICIJ investigation exposes a rogue offshore industry', Available at https://www.icij.org/blog/2016/04/new-icij-investigation-exposes-rogue-offshore-industry/. Accessed 30/12/2017.

ICIJ, 2017, 'But Where Is Bermuda, Luxembourg? New EU "Blacklist" Omits Major Tax Havens', Available at www.icij.org/investigations/paradise-papers/bermuda-luxembourg-new-eu-blacklist-omits-major-tax-havens/. Accessed 30/12/2017.

Institute of Business Ethics, 2017, 'Attitudes of the British Public to Business Ethics 2017', Available at www.ibe.org.uk/userassets/briefings/ibe_survey_attitudes_of_the_british_public_to_business_ethics_2017.pdf. Accessed 30/12/2017.

Ioannou, I. and Serafeim, G., 2017, 'The Consequences of Mandatory Corporate Sustainability Reporting', Harvard Business School Research Working Paper (11–100). Available at https://papers.ssrn.com/sol3/papers.cfm?abstract_id=1799589. Accessed 08/06/2019.

Jolly, D., 2014, 'Criticized on Taxes, Starbucks Will Move European Offices to London', *New York Times*. Available at www.nytimes.com/2014/04/17/business/international/starbucks-to-move-european-offices-to-london.html. Accessed 30/12/2017.

Kocieniewski, D., 2011, 'G. E.'s Strategies Let It Avoid Taxes Altogether', *New York Times*. Available at www.nytimes.com/2011/03/25/business/economy/25tax.html. Accessed 30/12/2017.

KPMG, 2017, 'The Road Ahead: The KPMG Survey of Corporate Responsibility Reporting 2017'.

Lanis, R. and Richardson, G., 2012, 'Corporate Social Responsibility and Tax Aggressiveness: An Empirical Analysis', *Journal of Accounting and Public Policy*, 31 (1), pp. 86–108.

Lanis, R. and Richardson, G., 2015, 'Is Corporate Social Responsibility Performance Associated with Tax Avoidance?', *Journal of Business Ethics*, 127 (2), pp. 439–457.

Ministère des Affaires Etrangères – France, 2012, 'The French Legislation on Extra-Financial Reporting: Built on Consensus', Available at www.diplomatie.gouv.fr/IMG/pdf/Mandatory_reporting_built_on_consensus_in_France.pdf. Accessed 07/08/2018.

Norman, W. and MacDonald, C., 2004, 'Getting to the Bottom of "Triple Bottom Line"', *Business Ethics Quarterly*, 14 (2), pp. 243–262.

OECD, 2015, 'OECD/G20 Base Erosion and Profit Shifting Project 2015 Final Reports: Information Brief', Available at www.oecd.org/ctp/beps-reports-2015-information-brief.pdf. Accessed 30/12/2017.

OECD, 2017, 'About the Inclusive Framework on BEPS', Available at www.oecd.org/tax/beps/beps-about.htm. Accessed 30/12/2017.

Pew Research Center, 2017, 'Top Frustrations with Tax System: Sense That Corporations, Wealthy Don't Pay Fair Share', Available at www.people-press.org/2017/04/14/top-frustrations-with-tax-system-sense-that-corporations-wealthy-dont-pay-fair-share/. Accessed 30/12/2017.

Preuss, L., 2010, 'Tax Avoidance and Corporate Social Responsibility: You Can't Do Both, or Can You?', *Corporate Governance*, 10 (4), pp. 365–374.

Reggelin, N.-A., 2017, 'Germany: Multinationals Faced Increasing Tax Compliance Obligations in 2017, Uncertainty Lies Ahead', *MNE Tax*. Available at https://mnetax.com/germany-multinationals-faced-increasing-tax-compliance-obligations-2017-uncertainty-lies-ahead-25330. Accessed 18/12/2018.

Süddeutsche Zeitung, 2014, 'Konzerne ertricksen sich in Luxemburg Milliarden an Steuern', Available at www.sueddeutsche.de/wirtschaft/luxemburg-leaks-konzerne-ertricksen-sich-in-luxemburg-milliarden-an-steuern-1.2206997. Accessed 30/12/2017.

Swedish Institute, 2016, 'Corporate Social Responsibility in Sweden', Available at https://sweden.se/business/csr-in-sweden/. Accessed 30/12/2017.

TCFD (Task Force on Climate-Related Financial Disclosures), 2017, 'Final Report: Recommendations of the Task Force on Climate-Related Financial Disclosures', Available at www.fsb-tcfd.org/publications/final-recommendations-report/. Accessed 08/06/2019.

Tschopp, D. and Huefner, R., 2015, 'Comparing the Evolution of CSR Reporting to That of Financial Reporting', *Journal of Business Ethics*, 127 (3), pp. 565–577.

VNK/1256/50/2014, 'Ohjeistus valtion enemmistöomisteisille yhtiöille maakohtaisten verojen raportointiin', Available at https://vnk.fi/documents/10616/358621/Ohjeistus++valtion+enemmist%C3%B6omisteisille+yhti%C3%B6ille+maakohtaisten+verojen+raportointiin+2014/69e63ff6-3db9-439f-93ea-4110abd752a3/Ohjeistus++valtion+enemmist%C3%B6omisteisille+yhti%C3%B6ille+maakohtaisten+verojen+raportointiin+2014.pdf. Accessed 07/08/2018.

Watson, L., 2015, 'Corporate Social Responsibility, Tax Avoidance, and Earnings Performance', *Journal of American Taxation Association*, 37 (2), pp. 1–21.

Williams, D. F., 2007, 'Tax and Corporate Social Responsibility: A Discussion Paper', *KPMG LLP*. Available at www.kpmg.co.uk/pubs/Tax_and_CSR_Final.pdf. Accessed 07/08/2013.

Legislation

Anti Tax Avoidance Directive, 'Council Directive (EU) 2016/1164 of 12 July 2016 Laying Down Rules against Tax Avoidance Practices That Directly Affect the Functioning of the Internal Market', Available at http://data.europa.eu/eli/dir/2016/1164/oj. Accessed 16/10/2018.

Directive on the Mandatory Disclosure and Exchange of Cross-Border Tax Arrangements, 'Council Directive (EU) 2018/822 of 25 May 2018 Amending Directive 2011/16/EU as Regards Mandatory Automatic Exchange of Information in the Field of Taxation in Relation to Reportable Cross-Border Arrangements', Available at http://data.europa.eu/eli/dir/2018/822/oj. Accessed 16/10/2018.

The EU Accounting Directive 2013, 'Directive 013/34/EU of the European Parliament and of the Council of 26 June 2013 on the Annual Financial Statements, Consolidated Financial Statements and Related Reports of Certain Types of Undertakings, Amending Directive 2006/43/EC of the European Parliament and of the Council and Repealing Council Directives 78/660/EEC and 83/349/EEC Text with EEA Relevance', Available at https://eur-lex.europa.eu/legal-content/EN/ALL/?uri=celex%3A32013L0034. Accessed 02/02/2019.

The EU Capital Requirements Directive (CRD IV), 'Directive 2013/36/EU of the European Parliament and of the Council of 26 June 2013 on Access to the Activity of Credit Institutions and the Prudential Supervision of Credit Institutions and Investment Firms, Amending Directive 2002/87/EC and Repealing Directives 2006/48/EC and 2006/49/EC Text with EEA Relevance', Available at https://eur-lex.europa.eu/legal-content/EN/TXT/?uri=celex:32013L0036. Accessed 08/06/2019.

'Directive 2014/95/EU of the European Parliament and of the Council of 22 October 2014 Amending Directive 2013/34/EU as Regards Disclosure of Non-Financial and Diversity Information by Certain Large Undertakings and Groups', Available at http://data.europa.eu/eli/dir/2014/95/oj. Accessed 30/12/2017.

Finance Act 2016, 'UK Government', Available at www.legislation.gov.uk/ukpga/2016/24/contents/enacted. Accessed 07/08/2018.

Recommendation on Tax Treaties, 'Commission Recommendation (EU) 2016/136 of 28 January 2016 on the Implementation of Measures against Tax Treaty Abuse', Available at https://eur-lex.europa.eu/legal-content/EN/TXT/?uri=CELEX:32016H0136. Accessed 18/10/2018.

Revised Administrative Cooperation Directive, 'Proposal for a Council Directive Amending Directive 2011/16/EU as Regards Mandatory Automatic Exchange of Information in the Field of Taxation', Available at https://eur-lex.europa.eu/legal-content/EN/TXT/?qid=1454056899435&uri=COM:2016:25:FIN. Accessed 16/10/2018.

'Sanctions and Anti-Money Laundering Act 2018', Available at www.legislation.gov.uk/ukpga/2018/13/contents/enacted. Accessed 17/10/2018.

2 Defining tax transparency

Introduction

This chapter distinguishes tax transparency from tax evasion, tax avoidance, tax aggressiveness and tax planning. We discuss the differences in various tax behaviours and activities of the company and provide definitions that help distinguish them from each other. Companies' tax behaviour can be characterised by the degree of legality and ethics. Therefore, in classifying companies' tax behaviour, we strive to answer the following questions: Is the behaviour legal and is it ethical? Does society see the behaviour as good or bad? We provide definitions and discuss differences between different tax behaviours. We define tax transparency as voluntary disclosure of tax-related issues by companies. We introduce our self-constructed metric for measuring tax transparency, including the disclosure of a firm's tax policies, tax payments, regional tax distributions and other tax-related information. We define tax transparency in terms of a range of information a company voluntarily provides in relation to tax issues. We do not claim that there is necessarily a direct link between tax transparency measured in terms of the amount of information and the quality of information. To be tax transparent would require that good quality information is disclosed and that information is correct, relevant and useful to stakeholders.

2.1 Differences between tax evasion, tax avoidance, tax aggressiveness, tax planning and tax transparency

In order to define our theoretical construct of tax transparency, we need to start by distinguishing between different tax activities in which a company engages through the course of its activities associated with planning corporate tax. In Chapter 2, we focus on corporate tax. For companies, corporate tax can be viewed as a burden in the form of cost that it has to pay for running its business. Companies which consider tax as a cost of doing business would be expected to minimise costs and hence engage in tax planning strategies. However, such uncollected taxes have larger societal, ethical and other stakeholder implications (Freedman, 2003; Landolf, 2006; Friese, Link & Mayer, 2008). For governments and the public, corporate tax is a source of revenue used for government spending.

The OECD (2019a) report shows that income from corporate tax remains a significant source of tax revenues for governments across the globe. In 2016, corporate tax revenues accounted for 13.3% of total tax revenues on average across the 88 jurisdictions for which data is available. The importance of corporate tax is greater in developing countries where the average it accounts for 15.3% of all tax revenues in Africa and 15.4% in Latin America, compared with 9% in the OECD.

Since the 1950s, corporate tax paid by companies has been declining (see Figure 2.1). Figure 2.1 shows that corporate income taxes constituted just over 2% of the US gross domestic profit in 2015, while in the 1950s, it accounted for nearly 6%. Recent research suggests that the EU and US have lost almost 20% of their potential corporate tax revenue due to artificial profit shifting by multinationals (Tørsløv, Wier & Zucman, 2017).

Taxes serve for the provision of public goods – e.g. education, national defence and public health care in society. Taxation not only pays for public goods and services; it is a key ingredient of the social contract between citizens and the state and is thus key to building an effective government (DFID, 2010). As opposed to the mainly voluntary CSR activities, paying taxes is a legal obligation for firms and as such is an unavoidable cost of doing business. Given the differences in tax rates globally, as well as exemptions and reliefs granted by governments,

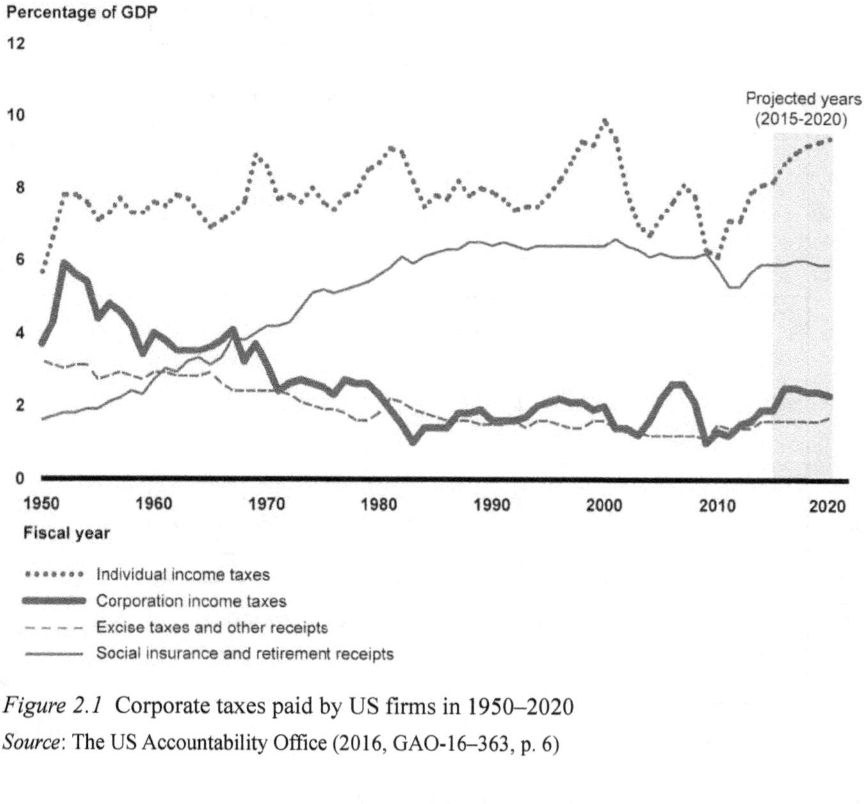

Figure 2.1 Corporate taxes paid by US firms in 1950–2020

Source: The US Accountability Office (2016, GAO-16–363, p. 6)

companies can pursue various strategies to minimise the tax they incur. Paying the minimum amount of taxes for a specific transaction required by law is a legal obligation, but tax planning and modifying the transactions can be used to alter the minimum. Tax avoidance strategies are usually based on taking advantage of differing tax rates in different countries, including the use of tax havens. The OECD has defined four key factors that identify a territory as a tax haven: (1) no or only nominal taxes, (2) lack of effective exchange of information, (3) lack of transparency and (4) no substantial corporate activities required (Preuss, 2010 p. 367).

The main distinction between tax activities performed by a firm lies in the degree of following the note of the law thus falling into legal or illegal tax activities. The second dimension is the perception of the tax activities as ethical or unethical, whether the society sees them as good or bad. Based on these two dimensions, we place all types of tax behaviour in the two-dimensional graph (see Figure 2.2). The dotted line in the graph represents the borderline between

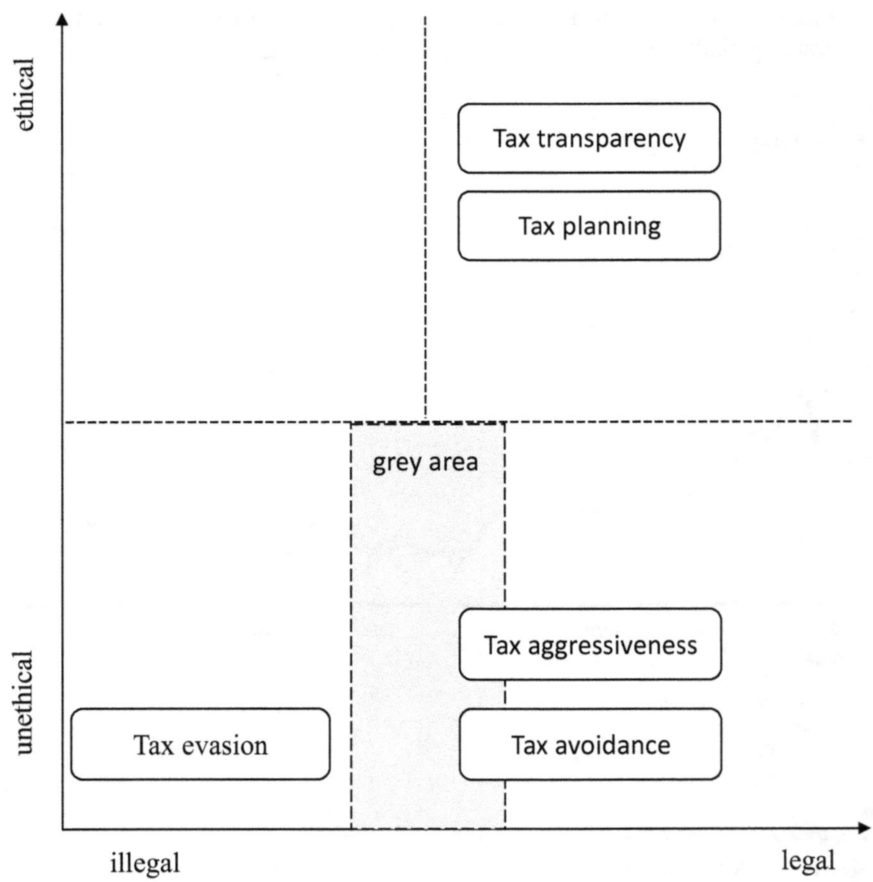

Figure 2.2 Differences between company's tax behaviour

unethical and ethical behaviour as perceived by the public. In this distinction, we do not address moral aspects of tax behaviour from a firm perspective (for review, see Prebble & Prebble, 2010). In certain cases, the behaviour is placed on the borderline, such as tax avoidance. It means that while the behaviour is technically legal, it exploits the loopholes in the tax system and hence lies in the grey area.

2.1.1 Tax evasion

Tax evasion is the process of illegally understating tax liabilities. In 2016, HM Treasury in the UK estimated that the existing tax system had a tax gap of around £40 billion (HM Revenue & Customs, 2016). One-sixth of this tax gap is estimated to be due to tax evasion. OECD defines tax evasion as "illegal arrangements where liability to tax is hidden or ignored, i.e. the taxpayer pays less tax than he is legally obligated to pay by hiding income or information from the tax authorities" (OECD, 2019b).

Hasseldine and Morris (2013, p. 6) define tax evasion as intentionally deceitful, corrupt or fraudulent behaviour that is against laws, whereas tax avoidance consists of legal means to optimise tax burden, usually to minimise taxes. The distinction is clear enough theoretically, and the condition of intentionality is important. If the intention of the company or tax consultants was to minimise taxes and they saw the action as being in line with existing laws (i.e. their interpretation differed from that of the tax authorities), the strategy cannot be classified as tax evasion.

A distinctive feature of tax evasion is that it is defined by the law and is prosecuted. The company that engages in tax evasion is acting both illegally and unethically. Since 2017, the UK recognises the facilitation of tax evasion as a criminal act under the new Corporate Criminal Offence (CCO) of Failure to Prevent the Facilitation of Tax Evasion legislation that came into force on 30 September 2017 as part of the Criminal Finances Act 2017 that applies to all companies. Under CCO, a company is likely to face unlimited fines if a person associated with it has enabled or facilitated tax evasion. To avoid conviction, the company must demonstrate that it has reasonable prevention procedures in place (EY, 2018).

Similarly, in Germany, tax evasion is classified as a serious criminal offence. If false financial records or annual financial reports lead to tax evasion, then the punishment is a fine or imprisonment up to five years (section 370(1), Tax Act). In cases of gross negligence, such failure is punishable with a fine of up to EUR50,000 (Oehmichen & Knierim, 2017).

2.1.2 Tax avoidance and tax aggressiveness

While tax evasion is completely illegal, the border between it and tax avoidance is blurred, and while not illegal per se, tax avoidance is charged with unethical connotations. In general, tax avoidance refers to a legal reduction in taxes (Gravelle, 2009). It can be equated to aggressive tax planning. It is not illegal but includes reducing tax liabilities by using tax law to gain a tax advantage. OECD (2019b) defines tax avoidance as "the arrangement of a taxpayer's affairs that is intended to reduce his tax liability and that although the arrangement could be strictly legal, it is usually in contradiction with the intent of the law it purports to follow". The premise for tax avoidance includes the loopholes between the national corporate taxation systems and the existence of tax havens. Both tax evasion and tax avoidance lead to BEPS. From a legal perspective, tax avoidance rests on the opportunity to achieve a mismeasurement of income which is overlooked in its creation, unjustifiable in its existence and intolerable to continue (Dixon, 2014). Tax avoidance and aggressiveness can be manifested as establishing subsidiaries in countries classified as tax havens or shelters (Col & Patel, 2019), debt restructuring (Nguyen, 2016) and transfer pricing (Bartelsman & Beetsma, 2003). From a societal perspective, tax evasion and tax avoidance contribute to the gap in corporate tax payments and undermine functioning tax systems that redistributes wealth and support the provision of public goods.

In Chapter 1, we discussed the rise of legislative forces to combat tax evasion and avoidance since the problem has a global scale. Recent tax avoidance scandals have attracted public attention. Similarly, scientific research corroborates that MNCs in general, and MNCs with more extensive foreign operations, have lower worldwide effective tax rates than other firms (Rego, 2003). Research using cross-country, firm-level data for a large sample of firms (1.2 million observations of MNE accounts) in 46 OECD countries finds that MNEs shift profits to lower-tax rate countries and that large MNEs exploit mismatches between tax systems and preferential tax treatment to reduce their tax burden (Johansson et al., 2017).

Literature uses tax avoidance and tax aggressiveness interchangeably. However, recent research into tax aggressiveness brings it closer to the notion of responsible corporate citizenship. Corporate citizenship generates an "obligation to pay tax in the jurisdiction within which the firm is operating" (Jenkins & Newell, 2013, p. 76). Tax aggressiveness "enables companies to enjoy the benefits of corporate citizenship without accepting the costs" (Amidu et al., 2016, p. 15). In Figure 2.2, tax avoidance and tax aggressiveness are placed in the unethical tax behaviour quadrant because tax aggressiveness is defined as "the pursuit of transactions and structures in order to reduce tax responsibility in a manner that is contrary to the policy or spirit of government legislation" (Bird & Davis-Nozemack, 2018, p. 1010). There is also an attempt to unite the two concepts into the term "aggressive tax avoidance". Aggressive tax avoidance is built upon an MNE's moral duty violation to obey the law; hence, it is understood as (Lenz, 2018, p. 4)

> the artificial (non-genuine) arrangement of transactions undertaken predominantly or exclusively by rational agents with the objective of tax optimization, meaning that it leaves the real value creation processes of the economic entities, i.e., the economic substance, largely unchanged. The agent's interpretation of law places little weight on the will of the democratically legitimized legislator, i.e., the intent or spirit of the law, and it dominates a mere literal interpretation, i.e., the letter of the law, which is extended to the boundary of what is likely to be just legally permissible.

Still on a semantic level, tax avoidance is viewed as being less criminal than tax aggressiveness. The lack of agreed understanding of what constitutes tax avoidance creates a problem. KPMG's Global Responsible Tax Initiative (2017) argues that if we do not have universal agreement on the definition of tax avoidance and tax aggressiveness, it becomes increasingly hard to draw the lines between aggressive avoidance and acceptable tax planning. There is no legal difference between a successful tax avoidance scheme and successful tax mitigation planning, each reduces the taxpayer's liability.

Research into the stock market reaction to tax aggressiveness finds that the market reacts negatively to the news of involvement in tax shelters (Hanlon & Slemrod, 2009). Firms that engage in excessive irresponsible CSR activities were found to have a higher likelihood of engaging in tax sheltering activities (Hoi, Wu & Zhang, 2013). At the same time, the market reacts positively to evidence that a firm is trying to reduce taxes when it can be deduced from the financial report that the firm is not tax aggressive. Recent attempts to understand the relationship between CSR and tax aggressiveness find that socially responsible corporations are likely to be less tax aggressive in nature. Amongst factors that reduce tax aggressiveness are social investment commitment and corporate and CSR strategy (including ethics and business conduct; Lanis & Richardson, 2012). At the same time, the challenge in quantifying the relationship between CSR and tax avoidance or tax aggressiveness stems from different proxies that are employed in research (Whait et al., 2018).

2.1.3 Tax planning

Every company engages in tax planning, and in Figure 2.2, it is defined as both ethical and legal. The main distinction between tax avoidance and tax planning is intent. While tax planning pertains to organising taxes in an efficient way that is suitable for the firm's strategy, tax avoidance exploits loopholes in the tax systems to the firm's benefit. Tax planning takes into consideration the strategy of the company and mitigates tax payments in a legal way. Still, we see that this distinction is far from ideal; a clear distinction would require comprehensive criteria and should be quantifiable. Tax planning service providers distinguish the difference by using risk as the main separating factor: "Tax avoidance always increases your tax risk, while tax planning either reduces it or does not increase your tax risk" (The Accountancy Partnership, 2016).

The blurry line between tax avoidance and tax planning remains the point of contention for enterprises, regulators and tax service providers. Currently, we do not have tools to measure the intent and company knowledgeability of the tax schemes beforehand.

2.1.4 Tax transparency

Tax transparency refers to the symmetry of information between tax authorities and tax payers (Hildreth, 2005, p. 429). We expand this definition of tax transparency by saying it is the condition when all tax relevant information is voluntarily provided by the company to a wide set of stakeholders. Tax transparency falls into both the legal and ethical domain as we define it in Figure 2.1. Tax transparency sets aside a company's voluntary disclosure of information on its tax issues. Tax transparency can be understood as a form of communication whereby the company shares its approach to taxes, its tax strategy and other tax-related elements it sees as relevant for stakeholders.

As discussed in Chapter 1, governments are increasingly demanding higher tax transparency from MNEs. At the same time, detailed tax information – e.g. satisfying OECD BEPS requirements – is only required to be submitted to governments. This stipulation is justified by the need to protect confidentiality, especially commercially sensitive information (Owens, 2014). MNEs do not have a legal obligation to disclose it to the public, except for the extractive and financial services industries in the EU. In our research, we observe that an increasing number of companies choose voluntarily to disclose tax-related information. We try to answer the following questions: How transparent are MNEs? What drives these companies to become transparent if studied through theoretical perspective lenses?

We also understand that placing tax transparency in an ethical domain can be questioned. Should a company be considered unethical if it uses legally allowed tax avoidance schemes but at the same time is voluntarily open about it through its transparent reporting on tax activities? These are questions to which there are no straightforward answers. However, what we can do is study the emerging phenomenon of voluntarily tax transparency and attempt to understand companies' motives and disclosure patterns.

Tax transparency has gained momentum due to public attention, tax scandals and regulatory attempts to curb tax evasion and tax avoidance. Tax transparency is gaining visibility in the EU and in the US by shedding light on tax secrecy and prompting more regulatory and tax authority oversight (Alexander, 2013). Similarly, Big-4 accountancy firms echo the need for increased transparency. For instance, EY (2019) states, "Increased tax transparency is inevitable", but at the same time points out the lack of a workable framework on reporting tax transparency. In EY's understanding, tax transparency consists of communicating the organisation's approach to tax planning and providing confidence to stakeholders that the organisation pays "a fair share of tax". Closely linked to it is the Global Responsible Tax Project by KPMG that brings together a range of stakeholders, including taxpayers, academia, media, government, global bodies, politicians, NGOs and tax professionals, to inform thinking on what responsible tax behaviour would look like in a global context. It covers discussions about who pays tax, how and when.

2.2 Tax transparency and CSR

Tax transparency is easily bridged with CSR due to the following reasons: (1) Both tax transparency and CSR are voluntary actions, and reporting on them is largely at the company's discretion. (2) Both are meant for communicating a company's internal information to a wider range of stakeholders rather than only shareholders who receive information primarily from financial reporting. A different question is whether tax transparency belongs to CSR reporting. In Chapter 1, we discussed the literature on whether tax can be considered part of CSR. The EU Accounting Directive (Directive 2013/34/EU, Chapter 10) made reporting on tax transparency compulsory from 2017 onwards for companies in the extractive industries that fall under the directive's scope. Hence, we observe that on one hand, tax transparency is voluntary and can be treated as part of CSR, but on the other, some industries face increased scrutiny and have to report detailed tax information (e.g. payments to governments on a CbC and a project-by-project basis).

Empirically, most studies have addressed the link between CSR and tax avoidance. A case study by Ylönen and Laine (2015) investigated how a company discussed taxation in its disclosures over a ten-year period as compared to its CSR claims. The results indicated that despite claiming to provide transparent communication, the company made only limited disclosures on taxation and issues such as tax planning, while tax risks and tax compliance had been omitted completely. The tension between tax transparency as part of CSR is noted in Dowling (2014) by drawing attention to examples where firms that "proudly proclaim" their social responsibility have been found to actively avoid paying corporate tax.

Few recent studies directly address tax transparency as part of CSR. Transparency of tax disclosures in corporate reports is found to be positively associated with IR (Venter, Stiglingh & Smit, 2017). Some studies advocated tax transparency as a new frontier in progressive CSR (Jenkins & Newell, 2013). On the European level, the European Business Network for Corporate Social Responsibility (2019) is launching a Blueprint on Tax Transparency and Responsible Tax Behaviour. The initiative tries to proliferate good practices and examples that companies can refer to in reporting on their tax transparency.

2.3 Measuring transparency in tax reporting

2.3.1 International standards

At present, there are few comprehensive guidelines or frameworks for transparent tax reporting. National or international financial reporting principles naturally require disclosing income tax figures. Additionally, the principle of materiality applies to any significant tax litigation or risks and hence companies would need to discuss these in their statutory financial statements. The UK requirement for the disclosure of tax strategy and the Finnish state-owned companies' tax reporting requirement can be seen as pioneering developments. The most influential CSR reporting guideline, GRI, gives reporters relatively high levels of choice to what extent and how to disclose payments to governments required under 201–1 (GRI, 2016). According to the latest GRI Standards 2016, under 201–1, in economic value distributed, payments to governments are defined as follows (GRI, 2016):

> An organization can calculate payments to governments as all of the organization's taxes plus related penalties paid at the international, national, and local levels. Organization taxes can include corporate, income, and property. Payments to government exclude deferred taxes, because they may not be

> paid. If operating in more than one country, the organization can report taxes paid by country, including the definition of segmentation used.

The guideline, hence, leaves it to the reporting organisation to decide whether to report taxes CbC, as well as what payments to include. Additionally, the standards do not offer an exhaustive list of the components to include in the figure and give no guidelines if the figure should be presented by payment type (e.g. CIT, property tax, penalties). It should, however, be noted that the direct economic value generated and distributed model is based on financial statements' profit and loss and hence payments to governments cannot include, for example, VAT collected. Yet regarding withholding taxes from employees' salaries, it is specifically stated that these should be presented in payments to employees (as opposed to payments to governments' component of economic value distributed). In any case, it is noteworthy that GRI does not simply focus on CIT but promotes a more comprehensive view of corporations' "tax footprint". In Chapter 5, we discuss the draft of GRI Standard on Tax and Payments to Governments that provides more comprehensive instructions on how to report on taxes if the topic has been deemed material.

Reflecting similar thinking, PwC developed the Total Tax Contribution Framework in 2005 with the goal of helping companies to communicate more fully the total contribution they make to government tax revenues (PwC, 2016). In order to facilitate clearer and more comparative reporting across companies, the framework categorises tax into five different bases (profit, people, product, property and planet) and makes a clear distinction between taxes borne (direct costs) and collected on behalf of governments (e.g. VAT collected). In this framework, CIT is only one component of the larger picture.

Corporate income taxes, in fact, make up a smaller portion of government revenue in comparison to personal income taxes, social contributions and consumption taxes (i.e. VAT, excise taxes), although the variation is significant across countries. In OECD countries, personal taxes were on average 24.4% of total government tax revenue in 2015, social contributions 25.8% and consumption taxes 38.4%, whereas corporate income taxes made up only 8.9% (OECD, 2017). Although corporations mainly simply collect consumption taxes and payroll taxes on behalf of governments, they bear significant costs for social contributions and pay consumption taxes for non-deductible expenses. Although CIT has been the bone of contention in the tax debate, it should be noted that it is not the only contribution that corporations make to government tax revenue. Yet the focus on CIT is certainly justified given that the possibilities for manipulating the tax cost are arguably widest, which can to some extent contribute to keeping its share of total tax revenue low.

2.3.2 *Tax transparency measurement in existing research*

We found little research comparing tax transparency between different companies through clearly defined measurement. A pioneering study in this field has been conducted by Hardeck and Kirn (2016), who constructed a comprehensive tax disclosure index (TDI) to facilitate their cross-country comparisons of the extent of tax disclosure in sustainability reporting. Their scoring model stems from the review of GRI G4 guidelines, OECD Guidelines for Multinational Enterprises, in addition to existing literature on tax-related sustainability reporting and actual reporting by companies. They include 21 items in 4 different categories ranging from "hard" (objective) numerical performance indicators to "soft" information on commitments to socially responsible taxation.

In order to measure tax transparency, we construct a five-point scale based on the number of tax issues discussed in CSR reporting. We measure the extensiveness of reporting in terms of the following aspects: sum of corporate income taxes, tax strategy, geographical spread of taxes, tax footprint and other (see Table 2.1).

The division into five categories stems from the existing guidelines regarding tax reporting presented earlier. Additionally, the categorisation is based on a review of tax matters in actual CSR reporting by MNCs and hence reflects the existing practice. A more detailed presentation of the scale used in our empirical research is included in Chapter 4.

Summary

The concept of tax transparency can be understood in relation to other types of tax behaviour that enterprises pursue during their lives. We provide definitions and examples from the research of tax evasion, tax avoidance, tax aggressiveness and tax planning. The main distinctive feature of these tax behaviours is the degree of following the law (legality) and of being ethical (how the behaviour is perceived by society). Tax evasion and tax planning are situated at the opposite ends of the legal vs. ethical continuum, with tax evasion being both illegal and unethical. Tax avoidance and tax aggressiveness are more difficult to place in that continuum. While technically legal, they may be against the spirit of the law and from the perspective of the wider stakeholder group be unethical. Tax transparency is an emerging concept that we define as companies' voluntary disclosures of its tax-related issues, often communicated via CSR disclosures but not limited to it.

Table 2.1 Tax transparency components and examples

Sum of corporate income taxes	*Tax strategy*	*Geographical spread*	*Tax footprint*	*Other*
Current tax expense or effective tax rate during the financial year	Characterisation of tax policy, company's and stance towards the use of tax havens	Income taxes by country or other geographical region (as defined by the company)	VAT, payroll taxes, property taxes	References to the societal importance of tax payments or the government's tax policy, self-characterisations, such as "major taxpayer"

References

The Accountancy Partnership, 2016, 'Tax Avoidance, Tax Planning and Tax evasion: What's the Difference?', Available at www.theaccountancy.co.uk/articles/tax-avoidance-tax-planning-tax-evasion-whats-difference-6316.html. Accessed 17/01/2019.

Alexander, R. M., 2013, 'Tax Transparency', *Business Horizons*, 56 (5), pp. 543–549.

Amidu, M., Kwakye, T. O., Harvey, S. and Yorke, S. M., 2016, 'Do Firms Manage Earnings and Avoid Tax for Corporate Social Responsibility?', *Journal of Accounting and Taxation*, 8 (2), pp. 11–27.

Bartelsman, E. J. and Beetsma, R. M., 2003, 'Why Pay More? Corporate Tax Avoidance through Transfer Pricing in OECD Countries', *Journal of Public Economics*, 87 (9–10), pp. 2225–2252.

Bird, R. and Davis-Nozemack, K., 2018, 'Tax Avoidance as a Sustainability Problem', *Journal of Business Ethics*, 151 (4), pp. 1009–1025.

Col, B. and Patel, S., 2019, 'Going to Haven? Corporate Social Responsibility and Tax Avoidance', *Journal of Business Ethics*, 154 (4), pp. 1033–1050.

Department for International Development (DFID), 2010, 'The Politics of Poverty: Elites, Citizens and States: Findings from Ten Years of DFID-Funded Research on Governance and Fragile States 2001–2010', Available at www.oecd.org/derec/unitedkingdom/48688822.pdf. Accessed 17/01/2019.

'Directive 2013/34/EU of the European Parliament and of the Council of 26 June 2013 on the Annual Financial Statements, Consolidated Financial Statements and Related Reports of Certain Types of Undertakings, Amending Directive 2006/43/EC of the European Parliament and of the Council and Repealing Council Directives 78/660/EEC and 83/349/EEC Text with EEA Relevance', Available at https://eur-lex.europa.eu/legal-content/EN/ALL/?uri=celex%3A32013L0034. Accessed 02/02/2019.

Dixon, D., 2014, 'Defining Tax Avoidance', *King's Student Law Review*, 5 (2), pp. 16–32.

Dowling, G. R., 2014, 'The Curious Case of Corporate Tax Avoidance: Is It Socially Irresponsible?', *Journal of Business Ethics*, 124 (1), pp. 173–184.

The European Business Network for Corporate Social Responsibility, 2019, 'Blueprint on Tax Transparency and Responsible Tax Behaviour', Available at www.csreurope.org/launch-event-blueprint-tax-transparency-and-responsible-tax-behaviour#.XH7tb4gzY2w. Accessed 06/03/2019.

EY, 2018, 'Criminal Tax Law: UK Corporate Criminal Offence (CCO)', Available at www.ey.com/Publication/vwLUAssets/ey-criminal-tax-law-UK-corporate-criminal-offence-cco-january-2018/$FILE/ey-criminal-tax-law-uk-corporate-criminal-offence-cco-january-2018.pdf. Accessed 12/01/2019.

EY, 2019, 'Tax Transparency: Seizing the Initiative', Available at www.ey.com/uk/en/services/tax/tax-transparency-report. Accessed 10/02/2019.

Freedman, J., 2003, 'Tax and Corporate Responsibility', *Tax Journal*, 695 (2), pp. 1–4.

Friese, A., Link, S. and Mayer, S., 2008, 'Taxation and Corporate Governance: The State of the Art', in W. Schön, ed., *Tax and corporate governance*, Berlin, Heidelberg, Springer, pp. 357–425.

Gravelle, J. G., 2009, 'Tax Havens: International Tax Avoidance and Evasion', *National Tax Journal*, 62 (4), pp. 727–753.

GRI, 2016, 'GRI Standards, Topic-Specific Standard GRI 201: Economic Performance 2016', Available at www.globalreporting.org/standards/gri-standards-download-center/. Accessed 18/05/2017.

Hanlon, M. and Slemrod, J., 2009, 'What Does Tax Aggressiveness Signal? Evidence from Stock Price Reactions to News about Tax Shelter Involvement', *Journal of Public Economics*, 93 (1–2), pp. 126–141.

Hardeck, I. and Kirn, T., 2016, 'Taboo or Technical Issue? An Empirical Assessment of Taxation in Sustainability Reports', *Journal of Cleaner Production*, 133, pp. 47–68.

Hasseldine, J. and Morris, G., 2013, 'Corporate Social Responsibility and Tax Avoidance: A Comment and Reflection', *Accounting Forum*, 37 (1), pp. 1–14.

Hildreth, W. B., 2005, 'Tax Transparency', in J. J. Cordes, R. D. Ebel and J. Gravelle, eds., *The encyclopedia of taxation & tax policy*, The Urban Institute, pp. 429–430.

HM Revenue & Customs, 2016, 'Annual Report and Accounts (2015–16)', Available at https://assets.publishing.service.gov.uk/government/uploads/system/uploads/attachment_data/file/537876/HMRC_Annual_Report_and_Accounts_2015-16-_print_.pdf. Accessed 12/01/2019.

Hoi, C. K., Wu, Q. and Zhang, H., 2013, 'Is Corporate Social Responsibility (CSR) Associated with Tax Avoidance? Evidence from Irresponsible CSR Activities', *The Accounting Review*, 88 (6), pp. 2025–2059.

Jenkins, R. and Newell, P., 2013, 'CSR, Tax and Development', *Third World Quarterly*, 34 (3), pp. 378–396.

Johansson, Å., Skeie, Ø. B., Sorbe, S. and Menon, C., 2017, 'Tax Planning by Multinational Firms', OECD Economics Department Working Papers. Available at www.oecd-ilibrary.org/economics/tax-planning-by-multinational-firms_9ea89b4d-en. Accessed 02/01/2019.

KPMG, 2017, 'The Global Responsible Tax Project: Different Ills Require Different Remedies: Is This True of Avoidance and Evasion?', Available at https://responsibletax.kpmg.com/page/different-ills-require-different-remedies-is-this-true-of-avoidance-and-evasion-1. Accessed 13/01/2019.

Landolf, U., 2006, 'Tax and Corporate Responsibility', *International Tax Review*, 29 (July), pp. 6–9.

Lanis, R. and Richardson, G., 2012, 'Corporate Social Responsibility and Tax Aggressiveness: An Empirical Analysis', *Journal of Accounting and Public Policy*, 31 (1), pp. 86–108.

Lenz, H., 2018, 'Aggressive Tax Avoidance by Managers of Multinational Companies as a Violation of Their Moral Duty to Obey the Law: A Kantian Rationale', *Journal of Business Ethics*, pp. 1–17.

Nguyen, H. K., 2016, 'A Review of Research on Corporate Tax Aggressiveness and the Leverage Puzzle', *Journal of Australasian Tax Teachers Association*, 11 (1), pp. 139–173.

OECD, 2017, 'Revenue Statistics: 1965–2016', Available at www.keepeek.com/Digital-Asset-Management/oecd/taxation/revenue-statistics-1965-2016_9789264283183-en#.Wkj-gE1lIiQ#page24. Accessed 31/12/2017.

OECD, 2019a, 'Corporate Tax Remains a Key Revenue Source, Despite Falling Rates Worldwide', Available at www.oecd.org/ctp/beps/corporate-tax-remains-a-key-revenue-source-despite-falling-rates-worldwide.htm. Accessed 15/01/2019.

OECD, 2019b, 'Glossary of Tax Terms', Available at www.oecd.org/ctp/glossaryoftaxterms.htm#E. Accessed 02/06/2019.

Oehmichen, A. and Knierim, T. C., 2017, 'Financial Crime in Germany: Overview', Available at https://uk.practicallaw.thomsonreuters.com/6-554-9114?transitionType=Default&contextData=(sc.Default)&firstPage=true&comp=pluk&bhcp=1. Accessed 02/06/2019.

Owens, J., 2014, 'Tax Transparency: The "Full Monty"', *Bulletin for International Taxation*, 68 (9), pp. 512–514.

Prebble, R. and Prebble, J., 2010, 'Does the Use of General Anti-Avoidance Rules to Combat Tax Avoidance Breach Principles of the Rule of Law: A Comparative Study', *Saint Louis University Law Journal*, 55, pp. 21–45.

Preuss, L., 2010, 'Tax Avoidance and Corporate Social Responsibility: You Can't Do Both, or Can You?', *Corporate Governance: The International Journal of Business in Society*, 10 (4), pp. 365–374.

PwC, 2016, 'The Total Tax Contribution Framework: Over a Decade of Development', Available at www.pwc.com/gx/en/services/tax/publications/total-tax-contribution-framework.html. Accessed 31/12/2017.

Rego, S. O., 2003, 'Tax-Avoidance Activities of US Multinational Corporations', *Contemporary Accounting Research*, 20 (4), pp. 805–833.

Tørsløv, T. R., Wier, L. and Zucman, G., 2017, '€600 Billion and Counting: Why High-Tax Countries Let Tax Havens Flourish', Working Paper. Available at https://static-curis.ku.dk/portal/files/185349685/TWZ2017.pdf. Accessed 11/01/2019.

United States Government Accountability Office, 2016, 'Most Large Profitable U.S. Corporations Paid Tax But Effective Tax Rates Differed Significantly from the Statutory Rate', *GAO-16-363*. Available at www.gao.gov/assets/680/675844.pdf. Accessed 10/12/2018.

Venter, E. R., Stiglingh, M. and Smit, A. R., 2017, 'Integrated Thinking and the Transparency of Tax Disclosures in the Corporate Reports of Firms', *Journal of International Financial Management & Accounting*, 28 (3), pp. 394–427.

Whait, R. B., Christ, K. L., Ortas, E. and Burritt, R. L., 2018, 'What Do We Know about Tax Aggressiveness and Corporate Social Responsibility? An Integrative Review', *Journal of Cleaner Production*, 204, pp. 542–552.

Ylönen, M. and Laine, M., 2015, 'For Logistical Reasons Only? A Case Study of Tax Planning and Corporate Social Responsibility Reporting', *Critical Perspectives on Accounting*, 33, pp. 5–23.

3 Drivers and theories behind tax transparency

Introduction

Various theories have been employed to provide rationales for companies' CSR initiatives and disclosures. These theories explain the increasing prevalence of CSR through the growth in the demand for CSR information and the benefits companies can gain from this additional disclosure. The stakeholder, legitimacy and institutional theories are socio-economic theories that draw on the fundamental assumption of the political economy framework. According to the political economy framework, "Society, politics and economics are inseparable and economic issues cannot meaningfully be investigated in the absence of considerations about the political, social and institutional framework in which the economic activity takes place" (Deegan, 2002, p. 292). Accordingly, by considering the aspects going beyond the purely economic and financial realm, the concept of CSR and the motivations behind CSR reporting can be more comprehensively understood. Additionally, this helps to account for possible variation across industries or countries. Agency theory, signalling and proprietary costs are economic theories that are useful for understanding factors resulting in the variance of amount and characteristics of disclosures across individual companies. Furthermore, implications of information overload theory to CSR and tax reporting are discussed. In this chapter, we go through each theory and concept and apply them to CSR and tax transparency, providing examples from tax disclosures.

3.1 Stakeholder theory

The stakeholder theory starts from the premise that corporations impact on and are influenced by multiple stakeholders that form the framework in which they operate. In addition to the most obvious groups, such as shareholders, customers, suppliers and employees, companies are also significantly linked to trade unions, NGOs, political groups, local communities, governments and the media.

3.1.1 Defining and identifying stakeholders

Stakeholders can be defined as "persons or groups that have, or claim, ownership, rights, or interests in a corporation and its activities, past, present, or future"

(Clarkson, 1995, p. 106). These rights or interests can be legal or moral, individual or collective and result from transactions with, or the actions taken by, the corporation (Clarkson, 1995, p. 106). Stakeholders who have similar interests, claims or rights can form groups, such as employees, customers or shareholders. If taken most broadly, the definition could comprise virtually everyone. Therefore, following Clarkson (1995), it is useful to distinguish between 'primary' and 'secondary' stakeholders. A primary stakeholder is "one without whose continuing participation the corporation cannot survive" (Sweeney & Coughlan, 2008, p. 114). Secondary stakeholders, on the other hand, are "those who influence or affect, or are influenced or affected by the corporation, but they are not engaged in transactions with the corporation and are not essential for its survival" (Sweeney & Coughlan, 2008, p. 114).

Mitchell, Agle and Wood (1997) identify power, legitimacy and urgency as three important stakeholder attributes that can be used to explain the priority managers give to competing stakeholder claims. The authors take power as "the ability of those who possess power to bring about the outcomes they desire" (Mitchell, Agle & Wood, 1997, p. 865). Regarding legitimacy, they follow Suchman's definition of legitimacy as "a generalized perception or assumption that the actions of an entity are desirable, proper, or appropriate within some socially constructed system of norms, values, beliefs, and definitions" (Mitchell, Agle & Wood, 1997, p. 866). The authors identify four bases on which legitimacy can be built:

1 The contractual relationship;
2 The stakeholder claim on the firm;
3 The stakeholder risk in the relationship; and
4 The moral claim – i.e. benefit, harm or rights violation.

(Mitchell, Agle & Wood, 1997, pp. 861–862)

The third attribute, urgency, is based on time sensitivity and the importance of the claim to the stakeholder. The authors point out that their theory is dynamic, and understanding how stakeholders can gain or lose salience to a firm's managers requires taking into account the following features as well: (1) Stakeholder attributes are variable, not steady state. (2) Stakeholder attributes are socially constructed, not objective reality. (3) Consciousness and wilful exercise may or may not be present (Mitchell, Agle & Wood 1997, pp. 867–868). One stakeholder may display various attributes to a different extent at different times. Furthermore, how managers perceive stakeholder attributes varies due to subjectivity. Therefore, managers' prioritisation of different stakeholder groups and the consequent attention and treatment of their claims vary accordingly.

In the case of taxation, governments are the most obvious stakeholders as the direct recipients of tax payments from corporations. States undeniably have the power to set up the legal framework for taxation, but the existing possibilities for tax avoidance, as well as cases of tax evasion, highlight the limitations and shortcomings in enforcement. The legitimacy of governments as stakeholders derives from the contractual relationship (i.e. legal obligation of companies to pay taxes), the direct claim (i.e. tax contributions), the stakeholder risk (i.e. states having inadequate funds to finance the functioning of governance and services) and moral claim (i.e. view that taxes are used by governments for the common good and harm is caused if companies avoid taxes). As societal services are funded from tax contributions, citizens can be seen as having a legitimate claim as well. So, for instance, media and NGOs aiming at providing citizens information or campaigning to guarantee that companies fulfil the claim are additional stakeholders. The salience is strengthened by the urgency of stakeholders' claims in the aftermath of the financial crisis that put governments in financial deficit and made the public more aware of the dependency of societal services from tax income.

3.1.2 Application of stakeholder theory

The stakeholder theory recognises the importance of balancing between, and preferably successfully aligning, the potentially converging interests of these various groups. The company's success and, ultimately, survival are at stake. Although the company's primary purpose is to make profit for the owners, shareholders are not necessarily seen as the primary stakeholders in the framework. Through different mechanisms, the company's profitability depends on satisfying the demands and expectations of customers, employees, media, government agencies etc. CSR can be seen as an integral part of the strategy to satisfy the demands of certain stakeholder groups, such as environmentally aware customers, investors pursuing ethical finance, NGOs advocating social causes or legislators assessing the need for additional regulation in labour matters (for example). It can be argued that from the point of view of these groups, CSR reporting is necessary since it enables the stakeholders to make informed decisions. Sweeney and Coughlan (2008) conclude, based on their empirical findings, that organisations in different industries report differently on CSR matters, and this variation is in accordance with the variation of key stakeholder expectations.

Donaldson and Preston (1995) have developed a taxonomy of stakeholder theory. Firstly, the theory can be descriptive, illustrating "whether and to what extent managers do in fact attend to various stakeholders and act in accord with their interests" (Margolis & Walsh, 2003, p. 279). Secondly, the theory can be normative and used for assessing "whether managers ought to attend to stakeholders other than shareholders and, if so, on what grounds these various stakeholders have justifiable claims on the firm" (Margolis & Walsh, 2003, p. 279). The theory can be employed instrumentally by managers to delineate and investigate the consequences (including economic benefits) that follow from attending to a range of stakeholders (Margolis & Walsh, 2003, p. 279).

3.1.3 Stakeholder approach in CSR reporting practice

The GRI framework emphasises the importance of stakeholder identification, and this reflects the stakeholder theory presented earlier. Stakeholder inclusiveness is the first of the four key reporting principles for defining report content.

The other three are sustainability context, materiality and completeness (GRI Standards, GRI 101: Foundation 2016). According to the standards, "[t]he reporting organization shall identify its stakeholders, and explain how it has responded to their reasonable expectations and interests" (GRI Standards, GRI 101: Foundation 2016). More specifically, the standard disclosures 102-40-102-44 require companies to disclose the stakeholder groups identified (102–40), relevant collective bargaining agreements (102–41), process of stakeholder identification and selection (102–42), approach to stakeholder engagement (102–43) and key topics and concerns raised by stakeholders (102–44). The stakeholder dialogue should be used to determine the relevant, or material, content of CSR reporting. Given the prevalence GRI in CSR reporting, it can be argued that a significant number of organisations clearly and consciously approach their CSR reporting from the stakeholder point of view. In the GRI framework, material topics are those that (1) reflect the reporting organisation's significant economic, environmental and social impacts or (2) substantively influence the assessments and decisions of stakeholders. Following this principle, most organisations following GRI reporting include a so-called materiality matrix that displays the importance of the identified matters to stakeholders on one axis (external assessment) and the importance to the company (internal assessment) on the other. An example of this can be found in Figure 3.1.

Reporting should reflect the relative importance of material topics – i.e. those topics that are highly important both to stakeholders and the organisation's impacts should be more extensively covered in the reporting. In our empirical examination, taxation, tax policy or tax transparency are defined as individual material topics in some organisations' materiality assessments. In other cases, they might be covered under broader umbrella terms, such as economic/financial impacts or contribution to society. It is up to the consideration of the reporting organisation how to define the exact topics based on the materiality assessment (internal and external) conducted.

In our empirical examination, we can logically see a connection between the materiality assessment regarding taxation and the extensiveness of reporting. For example, the British communication services company WPP has identified the importance of tax policy as "high" in both internal and stakeholder assessment. Consequently, the company has covered the topic rather extensively in its CSR reporting: information given includes the identification of the value of tax payments to society, the total tax figure, tax policy and specification of taxes paid by tax type (WPP, 2016/2017). Another UK-based company Reckitt Benckiser has assessed that the importance of tax has increased from 2016 to 2017. Consequently, its disclosures on the topic have become more extensive. In 2017, the company published its tax strategy report in accordance with the UK Finance Act 2016 requirements. However, the tax strategy report includes not only the legally required information on the company's tax strategy but also numerical figures and the discussion of the importance of tax in relation to corporate responsibility (Reckitt Benckiser Group plc, 2017; Reckitt Benckiser Group plc, 2016)

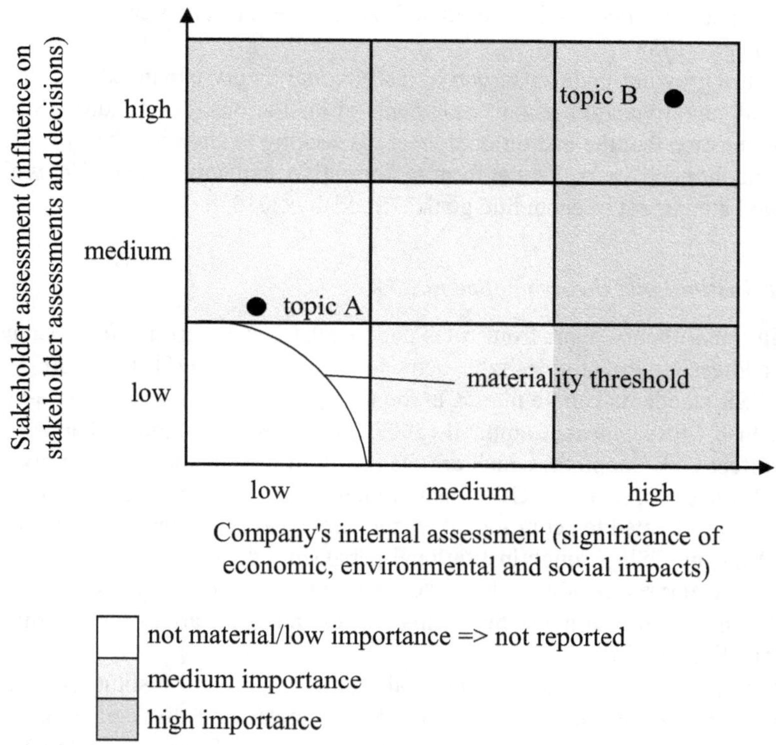

Figure 3.1 Materiality matrix

3.2 Institutional theory

Institutional theory originated in the 1970s and sought to uncover how social order is produced by social norms and rules that constituted particular types of actors (Meyer & Rowan, 1977). From an early institutional theory perspective, organisations were viewed as "'rationalised' systems – sets of roles and associated activities laid out to reflect means-ends relationships oriented to the pursuit of specified goals" (Scott, 2005, p. 465). Institutional theory deals with regulatory processes that establish rules for firms' behaviour and sanctions for violating it (Lawrence & Morell, 1995; Scott, 1995).

Institutional theory served to explain what makes organisations similar (DiMaggio & Powell, 1983) through a set of coercive and mimetic forces. Coercive or normative forces are represented by regulators, state and professional bodies, while mimetic forces come to play when organisations start to copy each other's behaviour. Initially, institutional theory viewed institutional environment and its elements (regulations, norms and associative forces) as top-down forces on the organisation (Scott, 1995). Later, bottom-up models of influence emerged where organisations themselves can be active players in setting the rules and norms and in a sense reflect their institutional environment through creative processes (DiMaggio, 1988).

With a growing body of research, institutional theory expanded into "softer" cultural cognitive and normative elements of institutions (Scott, 2008). Still, the main question that the institutional theory is seeking to answer is "why organizations adopt behaviours that conform to normative demands, but conflict with the rational attainment of economic goals" (Suddaby, 2010, p. 16).

3.2.1 Institutional theory applied to CSR

Institutional theory apart from rules and regulations governing firm behaviour also addresses norms for desirable behaviour (Suchman, 1995). Therefore, voluntary CSR standards can be placed in the category of norms for desirable behaviour. In a CSR context, Campbell (2007) identifies institutional characteristics that affect CSR adoption, which are the health of the economy, regulatory environment and presence of NGOs. Institutional theory is often used to explain why firms are motivated to act in socially responsible ways and engage in CSR activities. Viewing CSR through institutional perspective lenses, firms engage in corporate social responsibility to bring "corporate behaviour up to a level where it is congruent with prevailing social norms, values and expectations of performance" (Sethi, 1975, p. 62).

Institutional factors, such as political, cultural and legal institutions, may be contributing factors to differences in CSR practices and disclosures. Commitments to CSR were found to be different in companies from France, the Netherlands, the UK and the US (Maignan & Ralston, 2002) that can be explained by the degree to which stakeholders can influence the companies. Taking into considerations differences in nature of the companies and the political, financial, education and labour, coordination and control systems in Europe and USA, Matten and Moon (2008) suggest a model of "explicit" and "implicit" CSR. Implicit CSR is motivated by societal consensus and consists of values, norms and rules that result in (often codified and mandatory) requirements for corporations. Explicit CSR can be defined as more proactive corporate activities that assume responsibility for the interests of society, consists of voluntary corporate policies, programmes and strategies. In explicit CSR, the firm's objective is to meet expectations of different types of stakeholders. In Chapter 1, we provided analysis of legislative forces that shape CSR and tax transparency development in the world. Similarly, we can frame this discussion from an institutional theory perspective.

Coercive isomorphism regarding CSR includes codified rules and standards (e.g. GRI, EITI) and laws (e.g. EU directives transferred to national legislation) that shape CSR reporting practices. The EU has visibly engaged in multiple initiatives to foster CSR in Europe (Eberhard-Harribey, 2006). Expected compliance, for example, with the OECD BEPS project and EU Non-Financial Reporting Directive puts coercive pressures on companies to adopt practices in compliance with the new rules. Additionally, CSR-rankings and CSR-based investment funds put external pressures for CSR compliance and facilitate greater transparency in sustainability reporting. Normative isomorphism is reflected in inclusion of CSR in university curriculum and formation of CSR-related professional bodies (Matten & Moon, 2008). Formation of professional bodies and greater public awareness of CSR creates explicit pressures to adopt CSR. Finally, mimetic isomorphism can be understood as companies copying best practice or best behaviour. Most large companies would have a manager responsible for CSR and are likely to produce an individual or integrated CSR report refers to CSR becoming a more widespread practice over the years. Leadership-focused approaches to sustainability, such as the UN Global Compact (Williams, 2004) also reflect mimetic forces to which enterprises are subject. Mimetic processes are additionally operationalised by following similar reporting standards and copying best practices directly from reports.

Institutional theory gives grounds to legitimacy. According to Scott (2008), institutional regulative, normative and cultural-cognitive elements provide different rationales for claiming legitimacy, which can be achieved by legal sanctions, moral authorisation or cultural support.

3.2.2 Institutional theory and tax transparency

Discussion of different tax behaviours in which companies may potentially engage (tax planning, tax avoidance and tax transparency) falls into application of institutional theory in practice. Recent tax scandals and increased regulative emphasis on addressing tax avoidance is a good example. Regulative processes are easier to manipulate and change, but they often result in such behaviours as manipulation, "gaming" and decoupling instead of expected compliance (Evans, 2004; Roland, 2004). Tax regulations can be viewed as coercive power with which companies ought to comply. However, these rules are subject to interpretation and manipulation (Scott, 2008) that are likely to result in tax avoidance behaviour. The issuance of tax avoidance regulations per se is unlikely to result in the elimination of tax avoidance behaviour. From an institutional theory perspective, legal requirements shall be transitioned across normative and cultural-cognitive elements (Scott, 2008). This means that the shift from tax avoidance to tax transparency requires an understanding of "tax transparency" by professional bodies and by companies producing CSR reports. By investigating the emerging practice of tax transparency in reporting, we can see how this practice is unfolding and what cultural expectations corporations are facing.

Moreover, we observe a prevalence of bottom-up approaches when firms construct their vision of tax transparency in an institutional domain that does not have any prescriptive practices. At the same time, actors like GRI with its draft standard Tax and Payments to Governments and PwC with its total tax contribution framework are starting to develop best practices and guidelines for companies that want to address tax transparency issues. Furthermore, the initiative by KPMG's Global Responsible Tax Project seeks to create an inclusive stakeholder dialogue, including, for example, taxpayers, academia, media, NGOs and tax professionals to inform thinking on responsible tax behaviour in a global context (KPMG, 2019). Thus, we observe that CSR standards setters and Big-4 accounting firms are contributing to creating a normative base for transparent tax reporting. Mimetic processes are likely to be important when companies use tax transparency best practices from already published CSR or equivalent reports.

A practical example of a tax transparency reporting that sets the precedent for the best practices is a stand-alone tax footprint report by a Finnish-listed firm Fortum (see Table 3.1). Fortum has produced a tax footprint as part of its annual reporting since 2012.

In its tax footprint report, that is usually about ten pages long, Fortum comprehensively discloses total tax contribution, taxes borne and taxes collected. Taxes borne include corporate income taxes (excluding deferred taxes), production taxes, employment taxes, taxes on property and cost of indirect taxes that are reported in monetary value and a country basis. Items reported in the tax footprint

Table 3.1 Items reported in Fortum's tax footprint report 2017

Items reported in tax footprint report	*Description*
Total tax contribution	Taxes borne and collected in monetary value, reported by the three biggest production countries
Taxes borne	Corporate income taxes (excluding deferred taxes), production taxes, employment taxes, taxes on property and cost of indirect taxes reported in monetary value and as percent of total taxes borne. Reported on the country basis for the three biggest production countries and all others
Tax environment	Discussion on legal and other changes affecting tax (e.g. OECD BEPS, EU Commission's anti-tax avoidance directive)
Tax policy	Includes discussions on tax planning, tax risk management, tax governance (supported by an organisational chart), transparency and relationships with governments
Legal structure and intra-group financing	Examples of acquisitions and ownership restructuring, Q&A section on the role of financing and holding companies
Financial statement disclosures	Excerpts from income tax expenses, key tax indicators (effective income tax rate, weighted applicable tax rate, comparable effective income tax rate, total tax rate, comparable total tax rate) for the last three years, deferred taxes in the balance sheet
Tax indicators and CbC taxation	Key indicators that reflect the nature of its business operations and the related tax. Justification for selection of value creation base (as Fortum's operations are capital intensive and have a long lifetime, the net assets has been selected as the best determinant of our value creation in each country. Data reported on assets used in operations along with taxes borne and taxes collected for the 11 of the most significant countries of operation)
Other	Other payments to the public sector, ongoing tax appeals, information about companies registered in countries considered to be tax haven

Source: Fortum (2017)

report also include detailed tax policy, legal structure and intra-group financing, financial statement disclosures, tax indicators and CbC taxation and some other relevant tax-related issues. If firms began following Fortum's example, this would mean that mimetic processes are taking place in the sphere of tax transparency reporting.

3.3 Legitimacy theory

3.3.1 Defining legitimacy

Being a systems-oriented perspective, the legitimacy theory assumes that companies are influenced by, and in turn have influence upon, the society in which they operate. The idea of legitimacy derives from the concept of social contract, and it is assumed that "an organisation's survival will be threatened if society perceives that the organisation has breached its social contract" (Deegan, 2002, p. 293). Breaching social contract would occur if the surrounding society came to perceive that the company was not operating within the prevalent norms and expectations of society. These expectations can be explicit, such as laws and regulations, or implicit, such as community expectations (Deegan, Rankin & Vought, 2000). Practical consequences of breaching the social contract could include customers boycotting the company's products, suppliers cutting the supply of labour and materials, investors eliminating the supply of financial capital or governments setting increased taxes or fines or tightening regulations. Therefore, legitimacy can be seen as a resource on which an organisation's performance (financial and non-financial) is dependent.

Legitimacy has been defined in various ways, and Suchman (1995) argues that there are, in fact, two concepts: one strategic and another institutional. The strategic tradition adopts a managerial or instrumental perspective and emphasises the ways in which organisations attempt to garner societal support. The institutional tradition has adopted a more detached stance and focuses on examining how structures and agents mutually generate cultural pressures that shape organisations' behaviour (Suchman, 1995, p. 572). Suchman (1995, p. 574) himself adopts an inclusive definition of legitimacy: "Legitimacy is a generalized perception or assumption that the actions of an entity are desirable, proper, or appropriate within some socially constructed system of norms, values, beliefs, and definitions".

3.3.2 Legitimation strategies

Lindblom defines four ways (legitimation strategies) in which an organisation can obtain, repair or maintain legitimacy in case the social contract between itself and society (and/or selected powerful stakeholders) were to break down:

1 Communicating changes in the corporation's output, methods and goals which have been made in response to shifts in the relevant public's expectations.

2 Demonstrating the appropriateness of the output, methods and goals to the public through education and information.
3 The corporation associating itself with symbols having high legitimate status.
4 Seeking to adjust societal expectations of its performance to its present organisational output, methods and goals.

(Lindblom, 1993 cited in Bebbington, Larrinaga & Moneva, 2008, p. 352)

It should be noted that options 2–4 do not require an actual change in behaviour by the company but rather only a change either in relevant public's perceptions about its performance or a change in what is expected of the company (i.e. what makes it legitimate).

3.3.3 Legitimacy and CSR

The legitimacy theory, when applied to CSR, suggests that the desire to legitimise an organisation's operations is a significant motivation behind CSR activities. Abiding by the social contract can be seen as demanding more from companies in addition to fulfilling legal requirements. Certain groups in society (including stakeholders) seem to increasingly expect companies to improve their environmental performance or engage in community development. In the field of taxation, the public's sentiment seems to be in favour of companies to refrain from the use of aggressive (albeit legal) tax avoidance strategies and hence pay their 'fair' share to society.

Corporate disclosure policies, including CSR reporting, can be employed in legitimation as they "are considered to represent one important means by which management can influence external perceptions about their organisation" (Deegan, 2002, pp. 291–292). Similarly, according to Guthrie and Parker (1990, p. 166), accounting reports are social, political and economic documents that "serve as a tool for constructing, sustaining, and legitimising economic and political arrangements, institutions, and ideological themes which contribute to the corporation's private interests". As opposed to financial reporting, the content and form of CSR reporting is not legally regulated and does not require external verification. Therefore, it can be argued that companies have considerably more leeway to use CSR reporting in legitimisation, but the discretionary information in official financial reporting can similarly be employed.

3.3.4 Empirical research on link between legitimacy and CSR

In order to evaluate the theory in practice, the relationship between sustainability performance and disclosure has been empirically researched. Most research employing legitimacy theory assumes that there should be a negative relationship as companies would attempt to mitigate poor actual performance with more extensive positive disclosures in order to achieve or maintain positive public perceptions. This would be in line with Lindblom's legitimation strategies 2–4 (referred to earlier), which do not necessarily require a change in actual behaviour. However, it should be noted that high-performing companies would also have an incentive to communicate extensively about their performance, which would be in accordance with Lindblom's legitimation strategy 1. The concept of signalling, which will be discussed in more detail later in this chapter, points to a similar conclusion. Therefore, it is not surprising that empirical research has showed mixed and ambiguous results (Cho & Patten, 2007; Hummel & Schlick, 2016). In order to achieve more robust results, later research has distinguished between non-monetary and monetary information (Cho & Patten, 2007) and high-quality and low-quality information defined in terms of verifiability, comparability and consistency (Hummel & Schlick, 2016).

Cho and Patten (2007) found support for a negative relationship between performance and extent of disclosure from American companies' environmental reporting. Their research showed that although "poorer environmental performance leads to higher levels of disclosure, the results also provide evidence that the nature of such disclosures appears to vary with respect to the use of monetary and non-monetary information" (Cho & Patten, 2007, p. 646). Amongst companies operating in non-environmentally sensitive industries, the worse environmental performers provided more non-monetary environmental information than their high-performing peers (Cho & Patten, 2007, p. 646). Hummel and Schlick's (2016) research on European companies, however, revealed that high sustainability performance was positively connected with high-quality sustainability disclosure. This is in line with Lindblom's legitimation strategy 1 as high-performers can provide verifiable and consistent information (e.g. numerical figures) on their good performance in order to respond to public expectations on sustainability. In contrast, companies with poor sustainability performance provided more of low-quality information. Therefore, companies with poorer sustainability record seem to resort to legitimation strategies 2–4, providing non-verifiable claims without actual evidence of results.

3.3.5 Tax and legitimacy

Paying taxes can be seen as an important part of corporate legitimacy. Companies pay taxes in return for the state-provided services they use to operate, for example, security and rule of law, educated workforce and infrastructure. Revelations of tax avoidance (even if legal) can be seen by the public as breaches of the social contract and have a potential to erode the legitimacy and trust placed in companies. GlaxoSmithKline's chief executive Andrew Witty's comment illustrates this:

> I really believe one of the reasons we've seen an erosion of trust, broadly, in big companies is they've allowed themselves to be seen as being detached from society and they will float in and out of societies according to what the tax regime is.
>
> (Witty quoted in Clark, 2011)

Christensen and Murphy (2004, p. 39) conclude that tax avoidance "enables companies to become economic free-riders, enjoying the benefits of corporate citizenship without accepting the costs". Governments and the public can justifiably perceive this as breaching the social contract and, therefore, being unethical and contrary to the principles of corporate responsibility.

Based on our review of CSR reporting, several companies emphasise their role as responsible corporate citizens whose duties include tax payments (see examples in Table 3.2). Additionally, companies point out that in addition to paying taxes, they contribute to local economies and societies more widely as employers, educators and providers and buyers of goods and services as well.

These corporate statements can be seen as an attempt by corporations to build legitimacy through illustrating how they abide by the social contract and pay their

Table 3.2 Tax as part of responsible corporate citizenship

Company	*Country*	*Quote from reporting*
BT Group	UK	"Paying tax is one of the ways we contribute to society as a responsible business" (BT, 2017).
Ladbrokes	UK	"We recognise that tax revenue is vital to economic prosperity and social stability. We also recognise that our contribution to governments and national finances through the taxes we pay is important and significant" (Ladbrokes Coral Group, 2016).
Elisa	Finland	"By paying taxes and other public levies, we participate in the development of society as a whole. We are one of Finland's largest payers of corporate income tax" (Elisa, 2016).
Deutsche Post	Germany	"By paying taxes and other duties to federal, state and local authorities in many different countries, the Group also helps finance the maintenance and expansion of infrastructure" (Deutsche Post, 2016).
Johnson & Johnson	USA	"As the largest and most diversified health care company in the world, it is Our Credo obligation to 'be good citizens – support good works and charities and bear our fair share of taxes'" (Johnson & Johnson, 2016).
Royal Dutch Shell	The Netherlands/ UK	"Finally, we continue to play a positive role in communities and wider society. This includes providing employment, education and paying taxes. It is about being a good neighbour" (Shell, 2017).
Konecranes	Finland	"We make an impact on society by providing jobs and income for employees, by boosting local economies as an employer, provider and buyer of services and goods, as well as by being a significant taxpayer" (Konecranes, 2017).
Kone	Finland	"Creating wealth via taxes and employment" (Kone, 2017).

share of taxes – just like individual citizens. Interestingly, the idea of citizenship has been linked to CSR in general. Some companies, particularly in the US, have even titled their CSR reports (global) citizenship reports – e.g. Procter & Gamble, Oracle, Accenture, FedEx, Citigroup and Walt Disney.

3.4 Reputation risk management

3.4.1 Defining reputation

The reputation risk-management perspective on CSR emphasises the impact that CSR performance can have on organisations' reputations.

Organisational reputation has been assessed in terms of relative standing or desirability, quality, esteem and favourableness (Deephouse & Carter, 2005, p. 331). Reputation can be conceived from an economic/strategic management perspective as a resource or an intangible asset with the potential for value creation – for example, through enabling price premiums, lower cost of capital and labour loyalty. Alternatively, it can be viewed from a sociological perspective as the outcome of shared socially constructed impressions of an organisation. Therefore, reputations are both viewed as being formed on the basis of organisations' actions, as well as constructed by others through their perceptions of those activities (Bebbington, Larrinaga & Moneva, 2008, p. 341).

It is recognised that damages to reputation can have adverse financial effects on the company and, therefore, constitute a risk for its success. From a strategic perspective, companies need to dedicate efforts for countering damages to their reputation. According to this view, reputation can be managed by companies through the process of risk identification, assessment and actions to eliminate or minimise the occurrence or consequences of these risks.

Bebbington, Larrinaga and Moneva (2008, pp. 339–341) have noted five elements of reputation to which six prominent reputation ranking studies/indices seem to focus on

1 financial performance;
2 quality of management;
3 social and environmental responsibility performance;
4 employee quality; and
5 the quality of the goods/services provided.

Arguably individuals – e.g. managers, customers or investors – consider (consciously or sub-consciously) these very aspects when forming an opinion or evaluating an organisation's reputation. However, the degree of importance of each aspect depends on the individual and the context. Consequently, in order to manage reputation risks, managers would need to consider these different aspects but note that some would have more significant consequences to reputation, depending on the context in which the company operates.

It should, however, be noted that from the sociological point of view, reputation could be such "a complex notion that may be impossible to model and study in systematic manner" (Bebbington, Larrinaga & Moneva, 2008, p. 341). This suggests that managing it could also be impossible. However, surveys of corporate practice have identified reputation management as the most common role for public relations (Bebbington, Larrinaga & Moneva, 2008, p. 341). In order to assess the feasibility of reputation management, we will later look at the results of CSR-related experiments in particular. In any case, it is important to remember the sociological point and the limitations it poses to the effectiveness of reputation management: often, it may be difficult to forecast what the stakeholders' perceptions of certain actions will, in fact, be and how this contributes to the collective formation of reputation. This means that managers' actions may have unintended consequences on their organisation's reputation.

3.4.2 Differentiating between reputation and legitimacy

Researchers acknowledge that the concepts of reputation and legitimacy have significant similarities. Deephouse and Carter (2005, p. 330) recognise both "result from similar social construction processes as stakeholders evaluate an organization"; "have been linked to similar antecedents, such as organizational size, charitable giving, strategic alliances, and regulatory compliance"; and "an important consequence of both is the improved ability to acquire resources". Indeed, reputation and legitimacy are occasionally used interchangeably, but they are, nevertheless, two different concepts.

For instance, Deephouse and Carter (2005, p. 329) conclude that "legitimacy emphasizes the social acceptance resulting from adherence to social norms and expectations whereas reputation emphasizes comparisons among organizations". In other words, as Adams (2008, p. 367) points out, it has been argued that "legitimacy is more bimodal" (a company either is perceived as legitimate or not), while "reputation refers to the relative standing of organisations to one another" (meaning the companies can be set along a scale based on how good their reputation is).

However, Adams (2008, p. 367) argues that when it comes to CSR and CSR reporting, "legitimacy, like reputation, is subjective", "stakeholders make judgments about companies relative to one another" and the perceptions of what makes companies legitimate vary amongst different stakeholder groups. Even if legitimacy can be perceived as a scale as well, a more crucial differentiating factor is that the basis of which legitimacy assessments can be made. This basis can justifiably be determined as narrower than that of reputation assessments. Deephouse and Carter (2005, p. 332) follow Ruef and Scott's recommendation that "legitimacy assessments be restricted to those involving regulative, normative or cognitive dimensions". Reputation, on the other hand, can be assessed on these aspects but in addition on "virtually any attribute along which organizations may vary" that hence enable comparisons (Deephouse & Carter, 2005, p. 332). The authors offer a good example to illustrate this: the architectural merit of corporate headquarters' buildings could impact corporate reputation, but it would be difficult to argue that this has anything to do with legitimacy (Deephouse & Carter 2005, p. 332).

3.4.3 Implications of reputation risk management to CSR

From the strategic perspective, CSR performance can influence companies' reputations, and it seems that this impact is continually increasing in importance (we look at research results on the matter later). Consequently, Bebbington, Larrinaga and Moneva (2008, p. 341) suggest that one of the business drivers for CSR reporting is "to have a good brand and reputation" – i.e. CSR reports can be seen as a means that organisations use to manage their reputation risk. To illustrate this, certain authors have used Royal Dutch Shell's *The Shell Report 1998* addressing public concerns about the Brent Spa oil platform and the Ngoni people from the corporate responsibility point of view. Fombrun and Rindova (2000) emphasise the importance of transparency for reputation management. Hooghiemstra (2000) sees corporate social reporting as impression management. Benoit (1995) identified "image restoration strategies" from Shell's report through which the corporation attempted to regain legitimacy and/or reputation in society and the public's eyes. The strategies include denial, different ways of evading responsibility and different ways of reducing offensiveness of the event. The strategies aimed at avoiding responsibility include claiming the event/action occurred due to provocation, accident or good intentions. Additionally, the subject may try to portray the event/action defeasible and avoid being held accountable because of, for example, lack of information, volition or ability. The offensiveness of the event can be reduced by means of bolstering (directing attention to other positive aspects), minimisation, differentiation, transcendence (redefining the context or rationale of the offensive act), mortification (acknowledging responsibility and asking for forgiveness), attacking the accuser, offering compensation and promising to take corrective action. Given the similarities between the concepts of legitimacy and reputation, Benoit's strategies have been compared to Lindblom's legitimation strategies and significant overlap has been noted. Bebbington, Larrinaga and Moneva (2008, p. 352) summarise: "Each of these approaches to obtaining, repairing or maintaining legitimacy find parallels in Benoit's framework with the possible exception of the strategy of mortification". First, communicating changes that have been made in response to shifts in the relevant public's expectations (legitimation) is cognate with Benoit's corrective action. Other Benoit's response categories seem to embody legitimation strategy 2 (demonstrating the appropriateness of the output, methods and goals to the public) that does not necessarily require changes in behaviour. Legitimation strategy 3 (the corporation associating itself with symbols having high legitimate status, again even without actual conformity based on behaviour) can be argued to be most closely connected with Benoit's strategies of bolstering and transcendence that aim at reducing the offensiveness of actions. Finally, Benoit's strategies of differentiation and minimisation that aim at reducing the offensiveness of actions can be linked to legitimation strategy 4 (adjusting societal expectations of present performance). Table 3.3 summarises the comparison (Bebbington, Larrinaga & Moneva, 2008, pp. 352–353).

Empirical research has been conducted to test the connection assumed by theories between reputation and communication. McDonnell and King (2013, p. 387) find that "boycotted firms do significantly increase their prosocial claims activity after a boycott is announced", and the reaction is larger when the boycott is perceived more threatening (measured by media attention), when the firm has a higher reputation or when the firm engaged in more prosocial claims already before the boycott. As in the case of legitimation, CSR reporting could be viewed as a mere self-interested public relations exercise if the reporting does not correspond to actual policies, actions and results achieved. However, the audiences seem to be aware of this risk, as Vanhamme and Grobben (2009, p. 273) find that "the use of CSR claims in crisis communication is more effective for companies with a long CSR history than for those with a short CSR history, and consumer skepticism about claims lies at the heart of this phenomenon".

As part of their CSR materiality analysis, several companies point out the business relevance of CSR matters, often through the reputation effect. For example, in its analysis of stakeholder perspectives, Walmart (2017, p. 175) identifies rising emissions and temperature as a societal change and connects its business relevance to not only to the cost of energy and carbon but also to reputation. As part of its specific Reputational Risk Framework, Deutsche Bank (2016, p. 32) defines that failing to appropriately manage and counter environmental and social risks may lead to reputational and financial risks. Deutsche Bank (2016, p. 32) sees that

Table 3.3 Comparison of Lindblom's legitimation strategies and Benoit's image restoration strategies

Lindblom's legitimation strategy (legitimacy theory)	*Benoit's image restoration strategy (reputation risk management theory)*
1 Communicating changes in the corporation's output, methods and goals which have been made in response to shifts in the relevant public's expectations.	Corrective action (mortification)
2 Demonstrating the appropriateness of the output, methods and goals to the public through education and information.	Denial Provocation Defeasibility Accident Good intentions Attack accuser Compensation
3 The corporation associating itself with symbols having high legitimate status.	Bolstering Transcendence
4 Seeking to adjust societal expectations of its performance to its present organisational output, methods and goals.	Differentiation Minimisation

Source: Based on Bebbington, Larrinaga & Moneva (2008, pp. 352–353)

its reputation is "founded on the trust of clients, shareholders, employees, regulators, and the public".

3.4.4 The relationship between CSR, corporate reputation and consumer behaviour

A fair amount of research has been conducted on the impact of CSR performance on corporate reputation and customer behaviour. Mohr, Webb and Harris (2001) summarise experiments on the impact of CSR performance to consumer purchasing decisions conducted in the 1990s. Holmes and Kilbane (1993) found that cause-related marketing (i.e. company promising a donation to philanthropy) did not have significant impact on purchasing decision. On the other hand, Creyer and Ross (1996) found that customers demanded lower prices from companies perceived as unethical (but were not willing to pay more for a company perceived as ethical). Lafferty and Goldsmith (1999), Murray and Vogel (1997) and Handelman and Arnold (1999) found a positive relationship between corporate responsibility or ethics and customer attitudes and/or purchasing decision. Different proxies have been used to capture CSR performance, which may well explain the differing results (i.e. cause-related marketing vs. corporate ethics) (Mohr, Webb & Harris, 2001). In their own survey, Mohr, Webb and Harris (2001, p. 69) found that "consumers are more likely to boycott irresponsible companies than to support responsible companies". Additionally, consumers' beliefs about CSR are often inconsistent with their purchasing behaviour, but the relationship will be stronger the more knowledge consumers have about CSR issues and the more important they judge these issues to be (Mohr, Webb & Harris, 2001, p. 69). This emphasises the importance of reporting as a means of delivering information. As information on CSR topics has become much more easily accessible through the Internet and media coverage, NGO efforts and the spread of CSR reporting, it is interesting to look at more recent surveys on corporate social performance and public attitudes.

The Cone Communications CSR Study has surveyed American consumers' attitudes towards CSR since 1993. The 2017 study shows that the benchmark data reveals a growing positive impact of CSR on brand reputation, loyalty and affinity. In 2017, 92% of respondents said they had a more positive image of the company when it supports a social or environmental issue (Cone Communications, 2017, p. 11). Given similar price and quality, 89% of consumers would be likely to switch brands to one that is associated with a good cause (up from 66% in 1993) (Cone Communications, 2017, p. 12). Mirroring Mohr's earlier research, the survey shows a possible discrepancy between attitudes and actions: 88% agreed that they would stop buying products from a company that has irresponsible or deceptive business practices, but only 50% have done so in the past 12 months. Eighty-seven percent stated that they would buy a product with a social and/or environmental benefit if given the opportunity, but only 55% have purchased one in the past 12 months. The survey points out that "millennials are leading the pack in their expectations and actions of responsible businesses" and the group scores higher than others in the questions presented earlier (Cone Communications, 2017, p. 31). This suggests further growth in the importance of CSR to consumers. When assessing the results, it should, however, be remembered that the survey has been produced by a CSR communications company and surveys often suffer from social desirability bias (i.e. respondents giving the answer that they perceive as socially acceptable or desired by the interviewer). Despite the possible limitations, the Cone study results from over two decades indicate the rise in the significance of CSR over time.

3.4.5 Tax and reputation

The research on the impact of tax matters in particular on corporate reputation and consumer behaviour displays similar results as in the case of CSR in general. This is logical as we have earlier come into the conclusion that it is justified to view taxation as part of CSR. Hardeck and Hertl (2014, p. 309) found that aggressive corporate tax strategies (CTSs) diminish and responsible CTSs enhance corporate success with consumers. However, consistent with earlier experiments, "consumers are not willing to pay a price premium for products sold by responsibly tax-planning companies, but punish aggressively tax-planning companies by a slightly lower willingness to pay" (Hardeck & Hertl, 2014, p. 309). The authors point out that consumers' own attitudes are important moderating variables. This suggests that individual or national-level attitudes towards paying taxes affect the assessments on any specific corporation's reputation in case of revelations of tax avoidance.

In the aftermath of the Panama and Paradise Papers revelations, the sentiment of public, media and governmental representatives towards the revelations of tax avoidance seemed to be largely negative, and the schemes have been widely condemned. The revelations have negatively affected the reputations of the companies mentioned in the leaked information. Yet, as we described in Chapter 1, tax scandals facing individual companies occurred even before the large-scale leaks. The Starbucks case of 2012 illustrates the concrete consequences of the damage to corporate reputation: the company altered its tax policy regarding UK taxation in order to avoid customer boycott. After it was revealed in the media that the company had been paying no tax in the UK since 2009, some politicians and union leaders called people to boycott the chain (Thompson & Houlder, 2012). Although the company representatives attempted to point out the significant contribution made through offering employment, it subsequently moved its headquarters to the UK from the Netherlands, which was estimated to increase the taxes incurred in the UK (Jolly, 2014). Again, the case illustrates that negative revelations have direct and drastic consequences to reputation and possibly to customer behaviour as well. Yet the impact of constantly displaying responsible behaviour is more difficult to ascertain.

Examples of the application of Lindblom's legitimation strategies and Benoit's image restoration strategies can be found in companies' communications after revelations or media coverage on their tax practices. In Chapter 4, we look at how

Vodafone and Nordea address the media attention they have met in their CSR reporting.

3.5 Agency theory

Agency theory gained popularity from the 1970s and aimed to describe the relationship between a principal and an agent to whom the principal delegates work (Jensen & Meckling, 1976). Agency theory addresses two problems: What should be done when the objectives of the principal and the agent diverge? How will we know what the agent is doing? In principal-agent relationships, the amount of available information is different for the principle and the agent, which results in a phenomenon called information asymmetry. Moreover, the agent is likely to be opportunistic or pursuing self-interest (Williamson, 1975) and more risk averse (Shapiro, 2005).

In agency theory, the unit of analysis is the contract that governs principal-agent relationship, and agency theory seeks to understand how to design the most efficient contract that would minimise agency costs (Eisenhardt, 1989). Findings from agency theory studies are used in designing monitoring mechanisms and contracts between CEOs and shareholders. Positivist agency theory looks at the ways governance mechanisms (e.g. composition of board of directors) and contracts can be designed to limit self-serving behaviour of the agent (Eisenhardt, 1989). In agency theory, information is regarded as a commodity that can be purchased and monitored, for example, by budgeting and other formal information systems (Eisenhardt, 1989).

3.5.1 Agency theory and CSR

Amidu et al. (2016) document previous studies that apply agency theory to both CSR and tax. Most commonly, CSR activities of the firm under agency theory are linked to managers' opportunistic behaviour. Petrovits (2006) finds that firms time their philanthropic contributions to achieve earnings targets. Prior, Surroca and Tribó's (2008) findings confirm that unregulated companies use CSR strategically to disguise earnings management, while this finding does not hold for regulated companies. McWilliams, Siegel and Wright (2006) view CSR as a part of managerial career advancement, whereby managers use CSR to promote their careers or other personal agendas.

At the same time, some studies – e.g. Kim, Park and Wier (2012) – look into ethical concerns as an alternative motivation for CSR that drives corporate financial reporting. Using a set of proxies for measuring transparency and reliability of financial information they conclude that ethical concerns are likely to drive managers to produce high-quality financial reports. Managers' personal values, motives and choices affect corporate strategy formulation and hence political processes within a firm provide a channel whereby personal values may inform CSR (Hemingway & Maclagan, 2004). Literature on the link between agency and CSR investigates motives behind managers' actions and studies the relationship between financial reporting and CSR performance. Agency theory in relation to CSR has been used to study the relationship between the board of directors' composition and readiness to implement CSR. For instance, the role of independent directors regarding the publication of CSR information is typically assessed in the light of trade-offs between the benefits and the costs of CSR reports for shareholders' interests (García-Sánchez & Martínez-Ferrero, 2017).

3.5.2 Agency theory and tax

Under institutional theory, the separation of ownership and decision-making functions leads to management acting as an agent of the firm being responsible for decisions about taxes (Slemrod, 2007). Slemrod (2004) posits that risk-neutral shareholders would expect managers to pursue profit maximisation, which include opportunities to reduce tax liabilities. Compensation contracts between shareholders and the management can potentially be tied to tax-related outcomes, such as effective tax rate or after-tax corporation profitability.

Tax avoidance activities can be categorised as value maximising as they transfer wealth from the state to shareholders. The separation of ownership and control leads to a problem of opportunistic behaviour. Empirical investigation built upon agency theory often includes models that use data from financial statements and proxies of tax avoidance behaviour. Managers behave opportunistically by engaging in tax avoidance resulting in earnings manipulation and in resource diversion (Chen et al., 2010; Desai & Dharmapala, 2009). Tax avoidance can provide managers with justification for their opportunistic behaviour (Desai & Dharmapala, 2009). Kim, Li and Zhang's (2011) study investigating the relationship between tax avoidance and future crash risks supports the agency perspective of tax avoidance.

Hanlon and Slemrod (2009) find a negative market reaction to news about a firm's involvement in tax shelters, suggesting that investors are concerned about managerial diversion, tax shelter activity and tax avoidance. Tax haven structures allow managers to derive private benefits, such as financial expropriation through tunnelling or managerial slack, which goes against the interest of noncontrolling shareholders and beyond simple tax saving motives (Bennedsen & Zeume, 2017). Future research utilising agency theory in tax transparency can potentially investigate value relevance of disclosures associated with increasing tax transparency or look at the design of principal-agent contracts that use tax transparency as one of the managerial outcomes.

3.6 Signalling theory

Signalling theory originates from Spence's (1973) work on labour economics and relies on the concept of information asymmetry where signallers of information and receivers possess different amounts and degrees of information. Information asymmetry can be reduced by the party possessing information by revealing it to others or, in other words, signalling it to others. An example of a signal can be an observable action, such as information release that uncovers the hidden characteristics (or quality) of the signaller. Signalling builds on the assumption that sending a signal should be favourable to the signaller, indicating a higher quality of its products compared with its competitors (An, Davey & Eggleton, 2011).

While signalling was initially applied in seller/buyer relationship, where the seller of high-quality products has an incentive to signal the quality of his products to the buyer in order to justify a higher price, it soon found its application to the company setting. Due to information asymmetry, the management of the company possesses more information than investors. If the company of a higher quality does not signal its quality to investors, it may lose out in attracting investors to a lower quality company. Under the signalling hypotheses, a higher quality company would have incentives to highlight its superior quality to investors by signalling it. This signal must be confirmable with a company's actions after the information is released.

We can represent the signaller and receiver relationship graphically (see Figure 3.2). Under conditions of information asymmetry, a signaller may choose to decrease the asymmetry by sending a signal to a receiver. Signal quality is defined by the cost of signal (how costly it is to prepare it) and by the value of the signal to receiver. Alternatively, a receiver may choose to decrease information asymmetry by performing a search for additional information. The search would depend on the cost incurred and on the value of information. Despite a receiver's best effort to gain additional information, some of it may not be accessible in the public domain, and acquiring any further information would mean law infringement. Hence the quality of the signal is linked to the nature of information signalled: the signal is of high quality if the information signalled is of proprietary nature – i.e. normally available only to the company's insiders. We later discuss the role of proprietary information in relation to tax transparency.

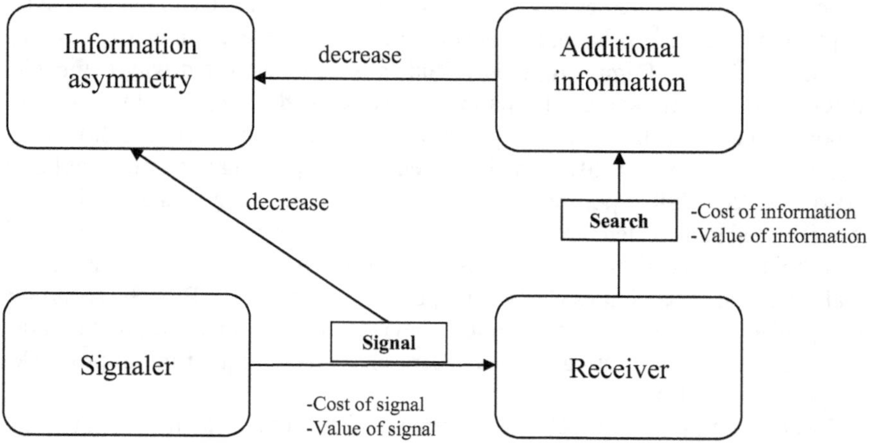

Figure 3.2 Information asymmetry and signalling

Source: Adopted from Karasek III and Bryant (2012)

Several studies look at examples of why companies choose to signal information. According to Inchausti (1997), owners are interested in giving good news to the market in order to avoid undervaluation of their shares. Companies can signal information about their reputations. Signalling theory predicts a relationship between size and disclosure. A larger company may have a greater incentive to signal its quality by means of improved disclosures (Craven & Marston, 1999). In accounting studies, signalling theory is often associated with voluntarily disclosures. Voluntarily adoption of IFRS standards is viewed as a means of reducing information asymmetry (Leuz & Verrecchia, 2000), as companies implementing IFRSs tend to display higher disclosure quality than their national GAAP (Daske & Gebhardt, 2006). Similarly, firms would have incentives to signal higher quality through IFRS reporting in order to obtain more debt and equity capital (El-Gazzar, Finn & Jacob, 1999). By following accounting standards with higher disclosure requirements, such as IFRS, companies can provide a positive signal to investors on their willingness to bridge the gap in information asymmetry (Tarca, 2004).

Watson, Shrives and Marston (2002, p. 291) examined why and which companies voluntarily disclose financial ratios, concluding that "If managers falsely try to signal that they are of high quality when in fact they are of low, once this has been revealed, no subsequent disclosures will be seen as credible". If a company discloses relevant information beyond what is required that becomes "best practice" and may signal quality. Thus, signalling theory predicts that higher quality companies choose accounting policies which allow their superior quality to be revealed. However, being caught signalling inaccurate and misleading information may result in a damaged reputation.

3.6.1 Signalling theory and CSR

Signalling theory addresses problems of information asymmetry in markets and is applied in the studies of voluntary accounting disclosure and voluntarily environmental disclosure (Campbell, 2004). Studies have investigated why companies disclose voluntarily some information in excess of that required by law. CSR reporting has been linked to the process of signalling corporate identity (Connelly, Ketchen & Slater, 2011) and is influential in improving corporate reputation (Pérez, 2015). CSR reporting itself can be viewed as a signalling mechanism, whereby a signal created through CSR reporting creates goodwill recognizable by stakeholders and can further have positive impact on reputation which is beneficial for economic activities (Galbreath, 2010; Shapira, 2012). By CSR reporting, companies can signal non-economic behaviour, such as their corporate values and culture, communicating social concern and unveiling their moral properties (Aqueveque, 2005).

Basdeo et al. (2006, p. 1205) view reputation forming as a signalling process "in which the strategic choices of firms send signals to observers and observers use these signals to form impressions of these firms".

Signalling through CSR reports influences corporate reputation through accountability for the past and future deeds, and firms that meet their stakeholders' expectations can gain in corporate reputation. However, unsubstantiated CSR communications not backed up by action or results can be labelled "greenwashing". Such communications can have a detrimental effect on a firm's reputation (Jahdi & Acikdilli, 2009). The quality of signal is paramount to the volume of information signalled, meaning signalling too much CSR information may not be the best strategy (Toms, 2002; Bebbington, Larrinaga & Moneva, 2008). A CSR communication as a signal is filtered through the stakeholder's perception and may result in either negative or positive impacts on reputation (Hetze, 2016). Widespread issuance of CSR-related disclosures means that an increasing number of companies want to signal their stance on CSR. Signalling, therefore, becomes the norm.

3.6.2 Signalling through tax transparency reporting

In order to understand the signalling process by means of tax transparency reporting, we use a concept of separating equilibrium (Bergh et al., 2014). Separating equilibrium occurs when participants weigh the returns and costs of investing in a signal and make optimising decisions with respect to the signal. In the case of tax transparency, this means dedicating effort in voluntarily producing public tax-related disclosures, for example, as part of CSR reporting. Equilibrium is achieved if the signal is confirmed – e.g. the company claiming to be tax transparent is not caught providing misleading information. Let us look at the stages of the equilibrium process:

1 An information problem exists

    In case of tax transparency, a belief may exist whether or not a company is tax transparent. Information about unethical tax avoidance is asymmetrically distributed. As demonstrated by recent tax scandals, the media reveals cases of unethical tax practice. Signallers interested in reducing information asymmetry on their tax behaviour would likely signal their tax-related information through voluntary tax disclosures.

2 Signal costs

    Signals are likely to reduce information asymmetry when they are costly to realise and imitate. Companies could be willing to produce tax-related disclosures because it is considered "best practice" amongst peers or as part image and reputation managing strategy. In case of tax transparency, we posit that companies may choose to disclose even bad news in order to avoid negative reputation costs and potential litigation in the future. This type of behaviour when managers may have legal incentives to disclose bad news in order to pre-empt large negative earnings was documented by Skinner (1994). Signalling cost of tax transparency of the company that has incurred reputational damage due to tax avoidance scandals would be disproportionately higher than the same effort of the company with an unstained reputation.

3 Pareto optimising solutions

Pareto optimising is achieved when there exists no other feasible solution for which an improvement for one party does not lead to a simultaneous degradation in one (or more) of the other parties. Using the same logic as in Spence's original labour market problem, the genuinely tax transparent company will earn the profits of being recognised as tax transparent, whereas the falsely tax transparent or tax opaque company will not. However, a pooling equilibrium where all companies signal may become possible in a hypothetical situation when tax transparency reporting becomes compulsory.

4 Signal confirmation

The final stage refers to a post-event situation and is an iterative process. Stakeholders will be satisfied if information is reliable and relevant; if the company demonstrates consistency; if other sources of information confirm the company's actions. Alternatively, inclusion of a company in, for example, Panama Papers or negative media coverage on tax avoidance may negatively affect trust in signalled information. As the penalty associated with false signalling increases, high-quality actors will be more likely to signal compared to low-quality actors.

Signalling theory originally views signal receivers as rational objects, but recently, a more behavioural perspective has been applied to signalling theory. Weick (1995) sees signalling through sensemaking lenses and explains that "a given signal from a given actor in a given environment takes on many different meanings owing simply to personality differences and variance in experiences across receivers". Information processing theory (Thomas & McDaniel, 1990) identifies a problem when several signals are produced so that the receivers may have challenges processing them all. In this situation, a solution includes producing a cruder signal that can be processed more quickly and effectively. Information processing theory is closely linked to the information overload discussion that follows.

3.7 Proprietary costs theory

Proprietary costs are the costs associated with revealing private information about companies. Proprietary costs are studied within empirical literature on disclosure choice since they have potential benefit for assessing firms' future profitability and are useful in firm valuation. By disclosing information that reduces information asymmetry, firms need to consider the costs of aiding competitors by revealing proprietary information (Ellis, Fee & Thomas, 2012). Disclosures to investors may include proprietary information that will also be observable to rivals. Therefore, managers decide whether to disclose such information by weighing conflicting objectives, reducing information asymmetry and avoiding proprietary costs related to informing competitors (Verrecchia, 2001; Hayes & Lundholm, 1996; Healy & Palepu, 2001). Graham, Harvey and Rajgopal (2005) found that executives were likely to favour limiting voluntary communication of financial information in order to prevent the firm from giving away company secrets or otherwise harming its competitive position.

Proprietary costs include the cost of preparing, disseminating and auditing information and disclosing firms' secrets (Verrecchia, 1983). The benefits of disclosing such information must outweigh these costs – e.g. by reducing the cost of capital. Suijs (2005) demonstrates that a firm's propensity to disclose bad news increases if it finds that the proprietary costs are higher than the disclosure costs. Proprietary costs may include the cost of regulatory action, potential legal liabilities, reduced consumer demand, damaged relationship with suppliers and other costs that negatively affect the firm (Dye, 1985). Moreover, proprietary costs can be divided into internal, including the cost of preparing and disclosing information and external costs that result from rivals using disclosed proprietary information to their advantage (Prencipe, 2004). The factors that affect decision to disclose information include industry-related factors and nature of competition. Additionally, the choice of the firm often follows industry rivals (Brown, Gordon & Wermers, 2006; Arya & Mittendorf, 2007). Ellis, Fee and Thomas (2012) find less information on the firms' customers is disclosed if a firm has larger R&D, greater level of intangible assets and larger advertising expenditures.

3.7.1 Proprietary costs in CSR context

Producing and providing voluntary environmental or social disclosures (e.g. information on environmental liabilities and risks or employee-related data) involves various proprietary costs (Verrecchia, 1983; Scott, 1994). This explains why all companies do not pursue CSR reporting despite recognising the potential benefits of doing so. For example, preparation costs occur because producing CSR reports requires additional labour resources and technical systems and possibly external auditing. Furthermore, there can be competitive costs since CSR reports may provide useful information to competitors to the disadvantage of the disclosing company. In this line of research, an observation is made that financial stability and capacity to invest in CSR reporting is needed for consistency of CSR reporting. Hence disclosing of proprietary information is only feasible for financially stable firms that can survive potentially negative consequences of revealing proprietary information (Cormier & Magnan, 2003; Cormier, Magnan & Van Velthoven, 2005). Ott, Schiemann and Günther (2017) demonstrated that firms' decisions to publish carbon disclosures depend on the environmental performance and the nature of the competitive environment (proprietary costs).

3.7.2 Proprietary costs and tax transparency

Tax information by its nature has long been considered confidential. While companies and individuals were obliged to report it to the tax authorities historically, tax information has been treated as confidential and not available to the public. With tax legislation reforms and increased voluntary tax transparency, tax information is gradually losing its exceptional status. The reasons for keeping tax information private and for making it available to the public are many but all built upon the premises of right to know and right to confidentiality.

The arguments for tax information disclosure include a general public right to tax, assumed link between tax confidentiality and tax evasion and creating social pressure for more accurate reporting (Schwartz, 2008). Exercising the pros and cons of publicly available tax return information, Lenter, Slemrod and Shackelford (2003) identify the following pros: aiding government regulators, improving the functioning of the financial markets, promoting tax compliance and increasing political pressure for good tax policy. The counter arguments against public tax disclosures are that disclosure would violate established norms of confidentiality and privacy and that it would create confusion and misinformation about corporate activities (Lenter, Slemrod & Shackelford, 2003). The same authors further develop their argument that disclosure of the entire corporate tax return could cause companies to dilute the information content of those returns and potentially reveal proprietary information. Generally, the confidentiality rule is supported by OECD BEPS requirements when tax-related information is only required to be submitted to the governments, and MNEs do not have an obligation to disclose it to the public. However, the industry-specific tax transparency initiatives (EITI and CRD IV in the EU) have established requirements for public CbC tax reporting in the extractive and financial sectors. In Chapter 5, we assess the proprietary costs related to public tax transparency reporting, for example, the CbC tax reporting legislation planned by the EU or tax footprint reporting promoted by the GRI.

3.8 Information overload theory

Information overload refers to the notion of receiving too much information from too many sources and is associated with related constructs of cognitive overload (Vollmann, 1991), communications overload (Meier, 1963), analysis paralysis (Stanley & Clipsham, 1997) and information fatigue syndrome (Oppenheim, 1997). Information overload occurs in different settings, such as information retrieval, organisation and analysis processes, decision-making processes and communication processes. There is no single generally accepted definition of information overload. The term is usually taken to represent a state of affairs where an individual's efficiency in using information in their work is hampered by the amount of relevant, and potentially useful, information available to them (Bawden & Robinson, 2009). Eppler and Mengis (2004) provide several definitions of information overload found in organisational sciences, accounting, marketing and related disciplines.

The origins of information overload can be traced back to the 1960s, but the phenomenon is exacerbated in our information society. The sources of information overload are increased use of ICT, advance of Internet and social media. In the current world, users are exposed to too much information they are not actively seeking. This affects their decision-making skills and leads to information fatigue syndrome (Edmunds & Morris, 2000). Eppler and Mengis (2004) identify five causes of information overload – namely,

1 organisational design,
2 the nature of information (e.g. the level of ambiguity, novelty and complexity),
3 the person involved in handling the information (e.g. attitude, qualification and experience),
4 tasks or processes to be completed (e.g. frequency of reoccurrence), and
5 the use or misuse of information technology like the Internet and e-mail.

In information overload theory, organisations and individuals are viewed as information processing systems. To demonstrate the effect of information overload, Schroder, Driver and Streufert (1967) developed an inverted U-curve model (see Figure 3.3) that relates information load to human information processing. Their model predicts that, in response to increases in information load, decision makers will increase their information processing initially. However, if information load keeps increasing and finally exceeds the capacity of decision makers, information processing will deteriorate. Too much information that is beyond decision makers' processing capacity will result in decreased decision accuracy and will lead to "information overload". At the same time, too little information will not result in optimal decision making; this phenomenon is referred as information underload.

In decision-making contexts, what matters is the relevance of information produced. It takes more time to separate relevant from irrelevant information, and often, additional information is sought to increase confidence. Ackoff (1967) warns of the danger of assuming that managers always need more information. Information has two dimensions: quantity and quality.

3.8.1 Quantity vs. quality debate

Quantity of information relates to the vast amount of information available on a particular topic and especially its rise due to Internet development. Quality of information is tightly linked with authorship; high-quality information would imply a trusted source and a recognised authority. Information dimensions include the number of different dimensions and the number of repeated dimensions. The number of different dimensions or 'information diversity' in a cue set represents the absolute diversity of the set, whereas the number of repeated dimensions or 'information repetitiveness' indicates the repetitiveness of the set (Hwang & Lin, 1999). The implication for information suppliers is that more is not always better in the case of information dimension. Even a moderate amount of increase

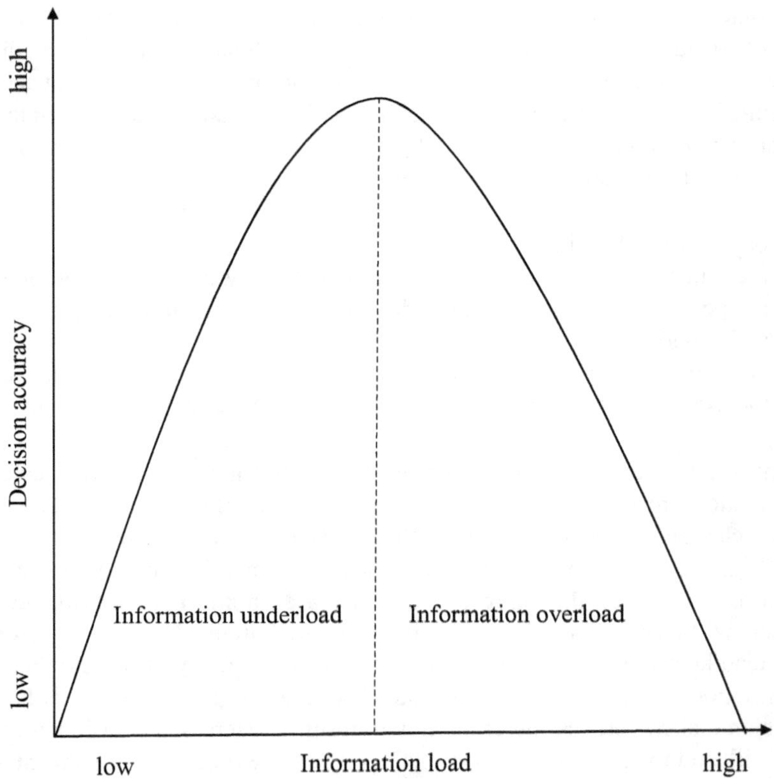

Figure 3.3 Information load and human information processing

Source: Adopted from Hwang & Lin (1999, p. 214)

in information dimension – e.g. an increase of information diversity from five to six – can hinder decision quality. Iselin (1988) demonstrated that in a highly structured task, the two information dimensions correlated with decision quality differently: diversity correlated negatively with decision quality, whereas the relationship between repetitiveness and decision quality followed and inverted U-curve (see Figure 3.3).

Since managers have a tendency to want as much information as possible, presenting just the right amount of information may be a challenging task for information suppliers (Hwang & Lin, 1999). Aldoory and Van Dyke (2006) demonstrated that participants in the experiment presented with too much information shut down cognitively. Bawden and Robinson (2009) describe how too much information results in information pathologies, such as information fatigue syndrome (Oppenheim, 1997), infobesity, information avoidance and information anxiety, that are all grouped under the title "paradox of choice". Too much information becomes a hindrance rather than a help, even though the information is potentially useful, and results in a loss of control over a situation and sometimes in feelings of being overwhelmed.

3.8.2 Information overload and CSR

Most MNEs provide CSR reports or disclose sustainability-related information on their websites. With a lack of worldwide accepted guidelines, these CSR reports vary in content, style and presentation from country to country, and even within the same industry, companies may have very different reports. While the most widely used standard for CSR reporting has been GRI, there are many additional standards and initiatives that contribute to the complexity of CSR comparison amongst companies (see the discussion in Chapter 1).

Neumann et al. (2012) warn of challenges that CSR and financial report users face by having to discern multiple information dimensions. They further comment that the increased number of CSR indicators and highly complex, subjective and voluminous non-financial information cannot be effectively used by stakeholders. Numerous CSR indicators and lengthy reports compete for the attention of different stakeholders and may lead to the inability to dissect the most relevant information. Large amounts of environmental information have been linked to the intention to influence the consumer (Bougherara, Grolleau & Mzoughi, 2007). However, increased access to information does not result in the ability to process it. Several data consolidators have resulted in the attempt to harmonise and increase comparability of CSR information. This resulted in ESG rating and environmental performance metrics provided, for example, by Worldscope Asset4 ESG database. Human information processing constraints are addressed by big data analysis and the advent of artificial intelligence (AI), which we discuss in more detail in the final chapter.

3.8.3 Information overload related to tax transparency

While many examples of information overload relate to the situations managers face, the same is true for stakeholders trying to make sense of tax-related information. Stakeholder ability to process information works in accordance with information overload principles.

External sources of information overload

First, the tax legislative framework, including tax shelters and tax havens arrangements, is creating ambiguities and information overload. Chapter 1 discussed the rapidly changing legislative framework that makes it difficult for stakeholders to keep track of whether the company is engaged in tax avoidance and if it is transparent enough. Second, two main leaks that contributed to tax transparency scandals both included an astonishing number of documents. In an overwhelming information environment where much information is released on an everyday basis, including media coverage of tax scandals and tax schemes, reliable tax disclosures provided by the company become highly relevant.

Internal sources

The lack of reporting framework on tax transparency issues contributes to information overload, as companies' tax transparency disclosures vary to a significant degree. The lack of consistency and comparability of tax information can create information fatigue and contribute to decision inaccuracies. This will be relevant, for instance, for funds managing socially responsible investments that include only tax responsible companies. Our research on the status of tax-related information in CSR reports shows that, usually, the amount is limited, if included at all. One exception is Vodafone, which has produced a separate tax report since 2012. The 2017 report consists of a respectable 82 pages. The report is structured carefully, having both summaries and detailed CbC information, which helps the reader to find the relevant information and avoid information overload.

Solutions

Solutions to information overload include common techniques, such as aggregation and summarisation. These techniques should be used to keep the number of information dimensions (both diversity and repetitiveness) to a minimum. Furthermore, the optimal number of information dimensions for each task should be determined empirically (Hwang & Lin, 1999). In the case of tax transparency, companies commonly understand the number of information dimensions needed for providing comprehensive tax position and tax strategy. It is possible to have data overload but not information overload:

> Data usually means a set of symbols with little or no meaning to the recipient. Information is a set of symbols that does have meaning or significance to their recipient.
>
> (Meadow & Yuan, 1997, p. 107)

New solutions will include identifying common factors that need to be presented by a company in order to report its tax position. In our tax transparency score, we include five elements: (income) taxes paid, tax strategy, geographical spread of taxes paid, tax footprint and other information that is not currently demanded by legislation as part of CSR reporting.

3.9 Summary of theories and their application to tax matters in CSR

Due to the evident interlinkages and overlaps, the stakeholder, legitimacy and institutional theories can be grouped together as 'socio-political' or 'socio-economic' theories. As Cotter, Lokman and Najah (2011, p. 87) summarise, each of the theories "suggests that social and/or political factors determine certain organisational behaviours including some voluntary disclosures". Additionally, the reputation risk management explanation can be linked with all these. Adams (2008, p. 367) states that there certainly seems to be "an overlap between: strategies to legitimize; strategies to minimise risk; and strategies used in engaging with stakeholders and a link between perceived reputation and legitimacy". Table 3.4 presents a summary of socio-economic theories by looking at underlying frameworks, key concepts, implications from the CSR point-of-view and implications from the taxation point-of-view and providing examples from related CSR disclosures.

As in the case of legitimation, CSR reporting could be viewed as a mere public relations exercise if the reporting does not correspond to actual policies, actions and results achieved. Additionally, being able to use CSR reporting for reputation risk management, the organisation would need to know what characteristics/actions/claims are perceived positively (either in relation to legitimacy or reputation) by different audiences (i.e. stakeholders). The institutional theory focuses on the context in which stakeholders form their opinions on the legitimacy and reputation of corporations. As Berrone and Gomez-Mejia (2009, p. 104) summarise, "The main thesis of institutional theory is that organizations enhance or protect their legitimacy (Scott, 1995) by conforming to the expectations of institutions and stakeholders (DiMaggio & Powell, 1983; Aldrich & Fiol, 1994)".

Applying the theories presented in Table 3.4 to tax issues as part of CSR suggests that societal pressures from different stakeholders and the surrounding formal and informal institutions impact on corporations' reporting. In order to succeed, companies need to be perceived by stakeholders as maintaining their social contract and on the other hand having a bad reputation can form a clear competitive disadvantage. Reputation is to a large extent created through communication (coherent actions may or may not be needed to back up the claims), and it can, in turn, impact on stakeholders' decision making. Legitimacy is particularly important for good reputation in the case of tax issues: paying taxes is an integral part of companies' side of the social contract. Showing taxes paid helps to build up companies' legitimacy in the eyes of stakeholders (consumers, employees, governments, civil society organisations, etc.). Particularly in the aftermath of the Panama and Paradise Papers, public trust in multinational companies to pay their 'fair' share of taxes has eroded. This is evident in the media coverage as well as intergovernmental initiatives, such as OECD BEPS, that aim to reveal corporate strategies and actions and counter tax avoidance. This can be seen as having created an institutional shift, both in the formal (i.e. legal and regulative actions) and informal sense (i.e. prevalent norms). As the significance of tax matters has risen for these stakeholder groups, it is not surprising that a larger number of companies has produced more extensive tax disclosures.

However, companies also communicate that government tax initiatives may harm their business: particularly the adverse impacts of environmental taxes or the financial transaction tax feature in the CSR reports. In doing so, companies seem to ask for understanding and acceptance of their lobbying efforts against

Table 3.4 Summary of socio-economic theories

	Stakeholder theory	*Legitimacy theory*	*Institutional theory*	*Reputation risk management*
Underlying framework	Political economy (social and political theories)	Political economy (social and political theories)	Political economy (social and political theories)	Reputation can be viewed as a sociological concept and from an economic point of view as a utilisable asset
Key concept	Stakeholder = "persons or groups that have, or claim, ownership, rights, or interests in a corporation and its activities, past, present, or future" (Clarkson, 1995, p. 106)	Legitimacy = "a generalized perception or assumption that the actions of an entity are desirable, proper, or appropriate within some socially constructed system of norms, values, beliefs, and definitions" (Suchman, 1995, p. 574)	Institution = established law or practice or a formal organisation, "cultural-cognitive, normative and regulative elements that, together with associated activities and resources, provide stability and meaning to social life" (Scott, 2001, p. 48)	Reputation = the shared socially constructed impressions of the entity, a resource/intangible asset with the potential for value creation (Bebbington, Larrinaga & Moneva, 2008, p. 341)
Implications from the CSR point of view	CSR activities are undertaken, and CSR disclosures prepared if the firm's management perceives that there is enough demand for these from important stakeholders.	CSR activities are undertaken, and CSR disclosures prepared in order to maintain social contract and hence guarantee organisation's survival.	The adoption and extent of CSR activities and CSR disclosures depend on the institutions in the environment where the company operates.	CSR activities are undertaken, and CSR disclosures prepared if this helps to build a good brand and reputation.
Implications from the taxation point of view	Taxation is particularly salient to these stakeholders: Governments as recipients of taxes have a direct interest. Increased media and public interest through revelations of MNCs' tax avoidance cases.	Complying with the social contract requires companies to pay taxes based on national legislation. However, companies and governments as well as the media and the general public may have differing views on the legitimacy of legal tax avoidance strategies. The breakdown of legitimacy may result in consumer boycotts, stricter tax regulations and intergovernmental initiatives to curb tax avoidance.	National legislation, law enforcement institutions, the media and NGOs, as well as general societal sentiments towards taxation, impact companies' tax strategies and reporting.	Revelations of tax avoidance can harm companies' reputations. This may form a disadvantage compared to competitors and cause adverse financial results.

Examples from disclosures	Tax-related matters identified as a material topics for stakeholders (or specific stakeholder groups) in materiality analysis. For example, direct taxes and other payments to governments are identified as key topic to stakeholder group 'society' by Kone (Kone, 2017, p. 11).	"Transparency and openness are key components to earn trust from society. During the year, Nordea has encountered incidents that bruised our customers' trust in us. In April, Nordea was pointed out as one of several actors in the "Panama Papers", where the media portrayed financial advice given regarding tax structures as unethical" (Nordea, 2016, p. 5). "Paying taxes is one way contribute to society as a responsible business" (BT, 2016, p. 24).	"In 2016, the UK government introduced a requirement for large companies to publish their Tax Strategy by the end of their 2017–18 financial year" (Vodafone, 2016–2017, p. 12).	"Our tax policy outlines our processes to identify, measure, control and report on risk across four categories: technical judgements, operations, regulations and reputation" (Prudential, 2017, p. 9).

Table 3.5 Summary of economic theories and information overload theory

	Agency theory	*Signalling theory*	*Proprietary costs theory*	*Information overload theory*
Underlying framework	Economic theory	Economic theory	Economic theory	Information processing theory
Key concept	Agency relationship = a relationship in which a principal delegates work to the agent, who performs the work. Agency theory studies contract between these two parties (Eisenhardt, 1989)	Signal = an observable action, such as information release that uncovers the hidden characteristics (or quality) of the signaller. Signalling builds on the assumption that sending a signal should be favourable to the signaller (An, Davey & Eggleton, 2011)	Proprietary costs = the costs that are associated with revealing private information about the company	Information overload = "the point where there is so much information that it is no longer possible effectively use it" (Feather, 1998, p. 118)
Implications from the CSR point of view	CSR activities are undertaken, and CSR disclosures prepared if the CEO and board of directors' views on the value of CSR reports are aligned. CSR information is typically assessed in the light of a trade-off between the benefits and the costs of CSR reports for shareholders' interests.	CSR reporting itself can be viewed as a signalling mechanism, whereby signal created through CSR reporting creates goodwill recognisable by stakeholders and can further have positive impact on reputation and be beneficial for economic activities (Galbreath, 2010; Shapira, 2012).	Companies weigh the pros and cons of disclosing CSR information by considering proprietary costs associated with and risks of aiding rivals by disclosing proprietary information.	Companies shall consider balance of information disclosed in terms of quality vs. quantity for avoiding information overload.
Implications from the taxation point of view	Tax avoidance can provide managers with justification for their opportunistic behaviour (Desai & Dharmapala, 2009).	The tax transparency information needs to be of good quality and confirmed so that it will serve as a signal that adds value to the receiver.	Tax transparency information can be categorised as proprietary information and not disclosed.	Information overload manifests in rapidly changing tax regulations, tax scandals information and excessive tax-related disclosures by firms themselves.
Examples from disclosures	Usage of conditions in executive compensation contracts that are tied to tax.	Companies caught in tax scandals tend to signal their tax transparency through increased disclosure (e.g. Nordea).	"We do not publish information about tax payments at country level, as we classify this as confidential" (Linde AG, 2017). Many companies leave tax-related information out of their reporting without explanation.	Some companies – e.g. Fortum and Vodafone – produce separate tax reports in which they have to balance quantity vs. quality and relevance of information to stakeholders.

these taxes that might appear justified to some stakeholder groups for ecological or fiscal reasons. Furthermore, job creation is often emphasised as part of corporate citizenship. Companies justify their critique of excessive taxes through stating that the tax burden can, ultimately, hinder business development and therefore opportunities to provide employment. Following Lindblom's legitimation strategies, this can be seen as an attempt to adjust societal expectations through educating the stakeholders about the negative impacts of tax burden.

Cotter, Lokman and Najah (2011, p. 87) recognise that increase in company value may well be a consequence of socially responsible behaviour. They, however, argue that wealth maximisation is not a consideration in socio-political theories. On the contrary, our understanding of the socio-political theories, especially when synthesised with reputation risk management, argues that legitimation in the context of stakeholders and institutions is a mechanism to secure the company's survival and enhance its financial performance by means of having a good reputation and legitimacy as a responsible corporate citizen. We also presented certain more narrowly focused theories, such as agency, signalling and proprietary costs theories, that Cotter, Lokman and Nojah see as focused purely on wealth maximisation. We argue that these 'economic theories' are value-adding but alone are insufficient for explaining CSR and tax disclosures. We summarise economic theories and information overload theory in Table 3.5.

Summary

Economic theories are useful for explaining choices made by reporters in specific circumstances. For example, if there are conflicting pressures from different stakeholder groups, economic theories may help in explaining the choice of disclosing or not disclosing information or the content of disclosures in that particular circumstance. For instance, proprietary costs theory explains why CbC tax contributions may not be disclosed (due to giving out confidential information on a company's competitive position). However, the socio-political legitimacy theory explains why this reason for non-disclosure may be particularly stated in reporting: the company tries to legitimise its action and defend its reputation as it recognises that the action may be against the pressures from certain stakeholders that demand increased transparency. We see reputation risk management as a bridge between these socio-political and economic theories. On one hand, reputation is a sociological concept, and its formation is best understood in the light of socio-political theories. However, from the economic point of view, reputation is as an asset that can be used for value creation. Our review of developments in the global tax landscape shows the significance of tax scandals to companies' reputation through the underlying mechanisms of legitimacy, institutions and stakeholders. As a general consequence, we see tax emerging as a topic in CSR reporting with an increase in the volume of tax-related information. Economic theories can be best used for explaining decisions on disclosure in particular cases – e.g. in the presence of conflicting pressures from the socio-political environment. However, in our view, the explanations relying on socio-political and economic theories agree on the ultimate goal behind the actions of companies: preserving and increasing the value of the company.

References

Ackoff, R. L., 1967, 'Management Misinformation Systems', *Management Science*, 14 (4), pp. B-147–B-156.

Adams, C. A., 2008, 'A Commentary on: Corporate Social Responsibility Reporting and Reputation Risk Management', *Accounting, Auditing & Accountability Journal*, 21 (3), pp. 365–370.

Aldoory, L. and Van Dyke, M. A., 2006, 'The Roles of Perceived "Shared" Involvement and Information Overload in Understanding How Audiences Make Meaning of News about Bioterrorism', *Journalism & Mass Communication Quarterly*, 83 (2), pp. 346–361.

Aldrich, H. E. and Fiol, C. M., 1994, 'Fools Rush In? The Institutional Context of Industry Creation', *Academy of Management Review*, 19 (4), pp. 645–670.

Amidu, M., Kwakye, T. O., Harvey, S. and Yorke, S. M., 2016, 'Do Firms Manage Earnings and Avoid Tax for Corporate Social Responsibility?', *Journal of Accounting and Taxation*, 8 (2), pp. 11–27.

An, Y., Davey, H. and Eggleton, I. R., 2011, 'Towards a Comprehensive Theoretical Framework for Voluntary IC Disclosure', *Journal of Intellectual Capital*, 12 (4), pp. 571–585.

Aqueveque, C., 2005, 'Signaling Corporate Values: Consumers' Suspicious Minds', *Corporate Governance: The International Journal of Business in Society*, 5 (3), pp. 70–81.

Arya, A. and Mittendorf, B., 2007, 'The Interaction among Disclosure, Competition between Firms, and Analyst Following', *Journal of Accounting and Economics*, 43 (2–3), pp. 321–339.

Basdeo, D., Smith, K., Grimm, C. M., Rindova, V. and Derfus, P., 2006, 'The Impact of Market Actions on Firm Reputation', *Strategic Management Journal*, 27, pp. 1205–1219.

Bawden, D. and Robinson, L., 2009, 'The Dark Side of Information: Overload, Anxiety and Other Paradoxes and Pathologies', *Journal of Information Science*, 35 (2), pp. 180–191.

Bebbington, J., Larrinaga, C. and Moneva, J. M., 2008, 'Corporate Social Reporting and Reputation Risk Management', *Accounting, Auditing & Accountability Journal*, 21 (3), pp. 337–361.

Bennedsen, M. and Zeume, S., 2017, 'Corporate Tax Havens and Transparency', *The Review of Financial Studies*, 31 (4), pp. 1221–1264.

Benoit, W. L., 1995, *Accounts, excuses and apologies: A theory of image restoration strategies*, New York, State University of New York Press.

Bergh, D. D., Connelly, B. L., Ketchen Jr, D. J. and Shannon, L. M., 2014, 'Signalling Theory and Equilibrium in Strategic Management Research: An Assessment and a Research Agenda', *Journal of Management Studies*, 51 (8), pp. 1334–1360.

Berrone, P. and Gomez-Mejia, L., 2009, 'Environmental Performance and Executive Compensation: An Integrated Agency-Institutional Perspective', *Academy of Management Journal*, 52, pp. 103–126.

Brown, N., Gordon, L. and Wermers, R., 2006, 'Herd Behavior in Voluntary Disclosure Decisions: An Examination of Capital Expenditure Forecasts', Working Paper, University of Maryland, College Park.

Bougherara, D., Grolleau, G. and Mzoughi, N., 2007, 'Is More Information Always Better? An Analysis Applied to Information-Based Policies for Environmental Protection', *International Journal of Sustainable Development*, 10 (3), pp. 197–213.

BT, 'Delivering Our Purpose Report 2016/17', Available at www.btplc.com/Purposefulbusiness/Deliveringourpurpose/Downloads/2017/2017_BT_DeliveringOurPurposeReport.pdf. Accessed 13/01/2019.

Campbell, D., 2004, 'A Longitudinal and Cross-Sectional Analysis of Environmental Disclosure in UK Companies: A Research Note', *The British Accounting Review*, 36 (1), pp. 107–117.

Campbell, J. L., 2007, 'Why Would Corporations Behave in Socially Responsible Ways? An Institutional Theory of Corporate Social Responsibility', *Academy of Management Review*, 32 (3), pp. 946–967.

Chen, S., Chen, X., Cheng, Q. and Shevlin, T., 2010, 'Are Family Firms More Tax Aggressive Than Non-Family Firms?', *Journal of Financial Economics*, 95 (1), pp. 41–61.

Cho, C. H. and Patten, D. M., 2007, 'The Role of Environmental Disclosures as Tools of Legitimacy: A Research Note', *Accounting, Organizations and Society*, 32, pp. 639–647.

Christensen, J. and Murphy, R., 2004, 'The Social Irresponsibility of Corporate Tax Avoidance: Taking CSR to the Bottom Line', *Development*, 47 (3), pp. 37–44.

Clark, A., 2011, 'Andrew Witty of GSK: "Big Firms Have Allowed Themselves to Be Seen as Detached from Society"', *The Observer*. Available at www.theguardian.com/business/2011/mar/20/andrew-witty-glaxosmithkline-big-firms-detached-society. Accessed 16/04/2014.

Clarkson, M. E., 1995, 'A Stakeholder Framework for Analyzing and Evaluating Corporate Social Performance', *Academy of Management Review*, 20 (1), pp. 92–117.

Cone Communications, 2017, '2017 Cone Communications CSR Study', Available at www.conecomm.com/2017-cone-communications-csr-study-pdf/. Accessed 17/08/2018.

Connelly, B. L., Ketchen, D. J. and Slater, S. F., 2011, 'Toward a "Theoretical Toolbox" for Sustainability Research in Marketing', *Journal of the Academy of Marketing Science*, 39 (1), pp. 86–100.

Cormier, D. and Magnan, M., 2003, 'Environmental Reporting Management: A Continental European Perspective', *Journal of Accounting and Public Policy*, 22 (1), pp. 43–62.

Cormier, D., Magnan, M. and Van Velthoven, B., 2005, 'Environmental Disclosure Quality in Large German Companies: Economic Incentives, Public Pressures or Institutional Conditions?', *European Accounting Review*, 14 (1), pp. 3–39.

Cotter, J., Lokman, N. and Najah, N. N., 2011, 'Voluntary Disclosure Research: Which Theory Is Relevant?', *The Journal of Theoretical Accounting Research*, 6, pp. 77–95.

Craven, B. M. and Marston, C. L., 1999, 'Financial Reporting on the Internet by Leading UK Companies', *European Accounting Review*, 8 (2), pp. 321–333.

Creyer, E. and Ross, W. T. Jr, 1996, 'The Impact of Corporate Behavior on Perceived Product Value', *Marketing Letters*, 7 (2), pp. 173–185.

Daske, H. and Gebhardt, G., 2006, 'International Financial Reporting Standards and Experts' Perceptions of Disclosure Quality', *Abacus*, 42 (3–4), pp. 461–498.

Deegan, C., 2002, 'Introduction: The Legitimising Effect of Social and Environmental Disclosures: A Theoretical Foundation', *Accounting, Auditing & Accountability Journal*, 15 (3), pp. 282–311.

Deegan, C., Rankin, M. and Vought, P., 2000, 'Firms' Disclosure Reactions to Major Social Incidents: Australian Evidence', *Accounting Forum*, 24 (1), pp. 101–130.

Deephouse, D. L. and Carter, S. M., 2005, 'An Examination of Differences between Organizational Legitimacy and Organizational Reputation', *Journal of Management Studies*, 42 (2), pp. 229–360.

Desai, M. A. and Dharmapala, D., 2009, 'Earnings Management, Corporate Tax Shelters, and Book-Tax Alignment', *National Tax Journal*, 62 (1), pp. 169–186.

Deutsche Bank, 2016, 'Corporate Responsibility Report 2016', Available at https://www.db.com/ir/en/download/Deutsche_Bank_CR_Report_2016.pdf. Accessed 03/08/2018.

Deutsche Post, 'Seeing the Bigger Picture: Corporate Responsibility Report 2016', Available at www.dpdhl.com/content/dam/dpdhl/en/media-center/responsibility/dpdhl-corporate-responsibility-report-2016.pdf. Accessed 13/01/2019.

DiMaggio, P. J., 1988, 'Interest and Agency in Institutional Theory', in L. G. Zucker, ed., *Institutional patterns and organizations: Culture and environment*, Cambridge, MA, Ballinger.

DiMaggio, P. J. and Powell, W. W., 1983, 'The Iron Cage Revisited: Institutional Isomorphism and Collective Rationality in Organizational Fields', *American Sociological Review*, 48 (2), pp. 147–160.

Donaldson, T. and Preston, L. E., 1995, 'The Stakeholder Theory of the Corporation: Concepts, Evidence, and Implications', *Academy of Management Review*, 20 (1), pp. 65–91.

Dye, R. A., 1985, 'Disclosure of Nonproprietary Information', *Journal of Accounting Research*, pp. 123–145.

Eberhard-Harribey, L., 2006, 'Corporate Social Responsibility as a New Paradigm in the European Policy: How CSR Comes to Legitimate the European Regulation Process', *Corporate Governance: The International Journal of Business in Society*, 6 (4), pp. 358–368.

Edmunds, A. and Morris, A., 2000, 'The Problem of Information Overload in Business Organisations: A Review of the Literature', *International Journal of Information Management*, 20 (1), pp. 17–28.

Eisenhardt, K. M., 1989, 'Agency Theory: An Assessment and Review', *Academy of Management Review*, 14 (1), pp. 57–74.

El-Gazzar, S., Finn, P. and Jacob, R., 1999, 'An Empirical Investigation of Multinational Firms' Compliance with International Accounting Standards', *The International Journal of Accounting*, 34 (2), pp. 239–248.

Elisa, 2016, 'Annual Report', Available at https://corporate.elisa.com/attachment/content/Annual-Report-2016.pdf. Accessed 13/01/2019.

Ellis, J. A., Fee, C. E. and Thomas, S. E., 2012, 'Proprietary Costs and the Disclosure of Information about Customers', *Journal of Accounting Research*, 50 (3), pp. 685–727.

Eppler, M. J. and Mengis, J., 2004, 'The Concept of Information Overload: A Review of Literature from Organization Science, Accounting, Marketing, MIS, and Related Disciplines', *The Information Society*, 20 (5), pp. 325–344.

Evans, P., 2004, 'Development as Institutional Change: The Pitfalls of Monocropping and the Potentials of Deliberation', *Studies in Comparative International Development*, 38 (4), pp. 30–52.

Feather, J., 1998, *The information society: A study of continuity and change*, London, Library Association.

Fombrun, C. and Rindova, V., 2000, 'The Road to Transparency: Reputation Management at Royal Dutch/Shell', *The Expressive Organization*, 7, pp. 7–96.

Fortum Tax Footprint, 2017, Available at www.fortum.com/sites/g/files/rkxjap146/files/investor-documents/fortum_tax_footprint_2017_1.pdf. Accessed 01/06/2019.

Galbreath, J., 2010, 'How Does Corporate Social Responsibility Benefit Firms? Evidence from Australia', *European Business Review*, 22 (4), pp. 411–431.

García-Sánchez, I. M. and Martínez-Ferrero, J., 2017, 'Independent Directors and CSR Disclosures: The Moderating Effects of Proprietary Costs', *Corporate Social Responsibility and Environmental Management*, 24 (1), pp. 28–43.

Graham, J. R., Harvey, C. R. and Rajgopal, S., 2005, 'The Economic Implications of Corporate Financial Reporting', *Journal of Accounting and Economics*, 40 (1–3), pp. 3–73.

GRI, 2016, 'GRI Standards, GRI-101 Foundation 2016', Available at www.globalreporting.org/standards/gri-standards-download-center/. Accessed 18/05/2017.

Guthrie, J. and Parker, L. D., 1990, 'Corporate Social Disclosure Practice: A Comparative International Analysis', *Advances in Public Interest Accounting*, 3, pp. 159–176.

Handelman, J- M. and Arnold, S. J., 1999, 'The Role of Marketing Actions with a Social Dimension: Appeals to the Institutional Environment', *Journal of Marketing*, 63 (July), pp. 33–38.

Hanlon, M. and Slemrod, J., 2009, 'What Does Tax Aggressiveness Signal? Evidence from Stock Price Reactions to News about Tax Shelter Involvement', *Journal of Public Economics*, 93 (1–2), pp. 126–141.

Hardeck, I. and Hertl, R., 2014, 'Consumer Reactions to Corporate Tax Strategies: Effects on Corporate Reputation and Purchasing Behavior', *Journal of Business Ethics*, 123, pp. 309–326.

Hayes, R. M. and Lundholm, R., 1996, 'Segment Reporting to the Capital Market in the Presence of a Competitor', *Journal of Accounting Research*, 34 (2), pp. 261–279.

Healy, P. M. and Palepu, K. G., 2001, 'Information Asymmetry, Corporate Disclosure, and the Capital Markets: A Review of the Empirical Disclosure Literature', *Journal of Accounting and Economics*, 31 (1–3), pp. 405–440.

Hemingway, C. A. and Maclagan, P. W., 2004, 'Managers' Personal Values as Drivers of Corporate Social Responsibility', *Journal of Business Ethics*, 50 (1), pp. 33–44.

Hetze, K., 2016, 'Effects on the (CSR) Reputation: CSR Reporting Discussed in the Light of Signalling and Stakeholder Perception Theories', *Corporate Reputation Review*, 19 (3), pp. 281–296.

Holmes, J. H. and Kilbane, C. J., 1993, 'Cause-Related Marketing: Selected Effects of Price and Charitable Donations', *Journal of Nonprofit & Public Sector Marketing*, 1 (4), pp. 67–83.

Hooghiemstra, R., 2000, 'Corporate Communication and Impression Management: New Perspectives Why Companies Engage in Corporate Social Reporting', *Journal of Business Ethics*, 27, pp. 55–68.

Hummel, K. and Schlick, C., 2016, 'The Relationship between Sustainability Performance and Sustainability Disclosure: Reconciling Voluntary Disclosure Theory and Legitimacy Theory', *Journal of Accounting and Public Policy*, 35 (5), pp. 455–476.

Hwang, M. I. and Lin, J. W., 1999, 'Information Dimension, Information Overload and Decision Quality', *Journal of Information Science*, 25 (3), pp. 213–218.

Inchausti, B. G., 1997, 'The Influence of Company Characteristics and Accounting Regulation on Information Disclosed by Spanish Firms', *European Accounting Review*, 6 (1), pp. 45–68.

Iselin, E. R., 1988, 'The Effects of Information Load and Information Diversity on Decision Quality in a Structured Decision Task', *Accounting, Organizations and Society*, 13 (2), pp. 147–164.

Jahdi, K. S. and Acikdilli, G., 2009, 'Marketing Communications and Corporate Social Responsibility (CSR): Marriage of Convenience or Shotgun Wedding?', *Journal of Business Ethics*, 88 (1), pp. 103–113.

Jensen, M. C. and Meckling, W. H., 1976, 'Theory of the Firm: Managerial Behavior, Agency Costs and Ownership Structure', *Journal of Financial Economics*, 3 (4), pp. 305–360.

Johnson & Johnson, 'Health for Humanity Report: Progress in Citizenship & Sustainability', Available at www.jnj.com/_document?id=0000015c-ce37-df25-affd-eeb775760000. Accessed 13/01/2019.

Jolly, D., 2014, 'Criticized on Taxes, Starbucks Will Move European Offices to London', *New York Times*. Available at www.nytimes.com/2014/04/17/business/international/starbucks-to-move-european-offices-to-london.html. Accessed 30/12/2017.

Karasek III, R. and Bryant, P., 2012, 'Signaling Theory: Past, Present, and Future', *Academy of Strategic Management Journal*, 11, pp. 91–100.

Kim, J. B., Li, Y. and Zhang, L., 2011, 'Corporate Tax Avoidance and Stock Price Crash Risk: Firm-Level Analysis', *Journal of Financial Economics*, 100 (3), pp. 639–662.

Kim, Y., Park, M. S. and Wier, B., 2012, 'Is Earnings Quality Associated with Corporate Social Responsibility?', *The Accounting Review*, 87 (3), pp. 761–796.

Kone, 'Helping Cities Grow Sustainably: Sustainability Report 2017', Available at www.kone.com/en/Images/KONE_Sustainability_Report_2017_tcm17-72109.pdf. Accessed 13/01/2019.

Konecranes, 'Annual Report 2017', Available at www.konecranes.com/sites/default/files/investor/konecranes_annual_report_2017.pdf. Accessed 13/01/2019.

KPMG, 2019, 'The KPMG Global Responsible Tax Project', Available at https://responsibletax.kpmg.com/about. Accessed 15/03/2019.

Labrokes Coral Group, 'Corporate Responsibility Report 2016', Available at https://gvc-plc.com/wp-content/uploads/2018/03/ladbrokes-coral-cr-report-2016.pdf. Accessed 13/01/2019.

Lafferty, B. A. and Goldsmith, R. E., 1999, 'Corporate Credibility's Role in Consumers' Attitudes and Purchase Intentions When a High Versus a Low Credibility Endorser Is Used in the Ad', *Journal of Business Research*, 44 (2), pp. 109–116.

Lawrence, A. T. and Morell, D., 1995, 'Leading-Edge Environmental Management: Motivation, Opportunity, Resources, and Processes', *Research in Corporate Social Performance and Policy*, 1, pp. 99–127.

Lenter, D., Slemrod, J. and Shackelford, D., 2003, 'Public Disclosure of Corporate Tax Return Information: Accounting, economics, and legal perspectives', *National Tax Journal*, 56 (4), pp. 803–830.

Leuz, C. and Verrecchia, R., 2000, 'The Economic Consequences of Increased Disclosure', *Journal of Accounting Research*, 38, pp. 91–124.

Linde AG, 'Corporate Responsibility Report 2017', Available at www.the-linde-group.com/en/images/Corporate_Responsibility_Report_2017_en_tcm14-460543.pdf. Accessed 19/07/2019.

Maignan, I. and Ralston, D. A., 2002, 'Corporate Social Responsibility in Europe and the US: Insights from Businesses' Self-Presentations', *Journal of International Business Studies*, 33 (3), pp. 497–514.

Margolis, J. D. and Walsh, J. P., 2003, 'Misery Loves Companies: Rethinking Social Initiatives by Business', *Administrative Science Quarterly*, 48, pp. 268–305.

Matten, D. and Moon, J., 2008, '"Implicit" and "Explicit" CSR: A Conceptual Framework for a Comparative Understanding of Corporate Social Responsibility', *Academy of Management Review*, 33 (2), pp. 404–424.

McDonnell, M.-H. and King, B., 2013, 'Keeping Up Appearances: Reputational Threat and Impression Management after Social Movement Boycotts', *Administrative Science Quarterly*, 58 (3), pp. 387–419.

McWilliams, A., Siegel, D. and Wright, P., 2006, 'Guest Editors' Introduction Corporate Social Responsibility: Strategic Implications', *Journal of Management Studies*, 43 (1), pp. 1–18.

Meadow, C. T. and Yuan, W., 1997, 'Measuring the Impact of Information: Defining the Concepts', *Information Processing & Management*, 33 (6), pp. 697–714.

Meier, R. L., 1963, 'Communications Overload: Proposals from the Study of a University Library', *Administrative Science Quarterly*, pp. 521–544.

Meyer, J. W. and Rowan, B., 1977, 'Institutionalized Organizations: Formal Structure as Myth and Ceremony', *American Journal of Sociology*, 83 (2), pp. 340–363.

Mitchell, R. K., Agle, B. R. and Wood, D. J., 1997, 'Toward a Theory of Stakeholder Identification and Salience: Defining the Principle of Who and What Really Counts', *Academy of Management Review*, 22 (4), pp. 853–886.

Mohr, L. A., Webb, D. J. and Harris, K. E., 2001, 'Do Consumers Expect Companies to Be Socially Responsible? The Impact of Corporate Social Responsibility on Buying Behavior', *Journal of Consumer Affairs*, 35 (1), pp. 45–72.

Murray, K. B. and Vogel, C. M., 1997, 'Using a Hierarchy of Effects Approach to Gauge the Effectiveness of Corporate Social Responsibility to Generate Goodwill Toward the Firm: Financial Versus Nonfinancial Impacts', *Journal of Business Research*, 38 (2), pp. 141–159.

Neumann, B. R., Cauvin, E. and Roberts, M. L., 2012, 'Management Control Systems Dilemma: Reconciling Sustainability with Information Overload', in *Advances in management accounting*, Emerald Group Publishing Limited, pp. 1–28.

Nordea, 'Sustainability Report 2016', Available at www.nordea.com/Images/37-247009/Nordea_Sustainability_Report_2017_printable.pdf. Accessed 13/01/2019.

Oppenheim, C., 1997, 'Managers' Use and Handling of Information', *International Journal of Information Management*, 17 (4), pp. 239–248.

Ott, C., Schiemann, F. and Günther, T., 2017, 'Disentangling the Determinants of the Response and the Publication Decisions: The Case of the Carbon Disclosure Project', *Journal of Accounting and Public Policy*, 36 (1), pp. 14–33.

Pérez, A., 2015, 'Corporate Reputation and CSR Reporting to Stakeholders: Gaps in the Literature and Future Lines of Research', *Corporate Communications: An International Journal*, 20 (1), pp. 11–29.

Petrovits, C. M., 2006, 'Corporate-Sponsored Foundations and Earnings Management', *Journal of Accounting and Economics*, 41 (3), pp. 335–362.

Prencipe, A., 2004, 'Proprietary Costs and Determinants of Voluntary Segment Disclosure: Evidence from Italian Listed Companies', *European Accounting Review*, 13 (2), pp. 319–340.

Prior, D., Surroca, J. and Tribó, J. A., 2008, 'Are Socially Responsible Managers Really Ethical? Exploring the Relationship between Earnings Management and Corporate Social Responsibility', *Corporate Governance: An International Review*, 16 (3), pp. 160–177.

Prudential plc, 'Environmental, Social and Governance Report 2017', Available at www.prudential.co.uk/~/media/Files/P/Prudential-V2/reports/2017/esg-report-2017.pdf. Accessed 13/01/2019.

Reckitt Benckiser Group plc, 'Detailed Sustainability Report 2016', Available at www.rb.com/media/2469/rb-detailed-sustainability-report-2016.pdf. Accessed 15/01/2019.

Reckitt Benckiser Group plc, 'Sustainability Report 2017', Available at www.rb.com/media/3353/rb-sustainability-report-2017.pdf. Accessed 15/01/2019.

Roland, G., 2004, 'Understanding Institutional Change: Fast-Moving and Slow-Moving Institutions', *Studies in Comparative International Development*, 38 (4), pp. 109–131.

Schroder, H. M., Driver, M. and Streufert, S., 1967, *Human information processing*, New York, Holt, Rinehart and Winston.

Schwartz, P., 2008, 'The Future of Tax Privacy', *National Tax Journal*, 61, pp. 883–900.

Scott, T. W., 1994, 'Incentives and Disincentives for Financial Disclosure: Voluntary Disclosure of Defined Benefit Pension Plan Information by Canadian Firms', *Accounting Review*, 69 (1), pp. 26–43.

Scott, W. R., 1995, *Institutions and organizations: Foundations for organizational science*, London, A Sage Publication Series.

Scott, W. R., 2001, *Institutions and organizations* (2nd ed.), Thousand Oaks, SAGE Publications.

Scott, W. R., 2005, 'Institutional Theory: Contributing to a Theoretical Research Program', in K. G. Smith and M. A. Hitt, eds., *Great minds in management: The process of theory development*, Oxford, Oxford University Press, Ch. 22.

Scott, W. R., 2008, 'Approaching Adulthood: The Maturing of Institutional Theory', *Theory and Society*, 37 (5), p. 427.

Sethi, S. P., 1975, 'Dimensions of Corporate Social Performance: An Analytical Framework', *California Management Review*, 17 (3), pp. 58–64.

Shapira, R., 2012, 'Corporate Philanthropy as Signaling and Co-Optation', *Fordham Law Review*, 80 (5), pp. 1889–1939.

Shapiro, S. P., 2005, 'Agency Theory', *The Annual Review of Sociology*, 31, pp. 263–284.

Shell, 'Sustainability Report 2017', Available at https://reports.shell.com/sustainability-report/2017/. Accessed 13/01/2019.

Skinner, D. J., 1994, 'Why Firms Voluntarily Disclose Bad News', *Journal of Accounting Research*, 32 (1), pp. 38–60.

Slemrod, J., 2004, 'The Economics of Corporate Tax Selfishness', *National Tax Journal*, 57 (4), pp. 877–899.

Slemrod, J., 2007, 'Cheating Ourselves: The Economics of Tax Evasion', *Journal of Economic Perspectives*, 21 (1), pp. 25–48.

Spence, M., 1973, 'Job Market Signaling', *Quarterly Journal of Economics*, 87 (3), pp. 355–374.

Stanley, A. J. and Clipsham, P. S., 1997, 'Information Overload: Myth or Reality?', *IEE Colloquium on IT Strategies for Information Overload*. Available at http://digital-library.theiet.org/content/conferences/10.1049/ic_19971146. Accessed 01/06/2019.

Suchman, M. C., 1995, 'Managing Legitimacy: Strategic and Institutional Approaches', *Academy of Management Review*, 20 (3), pp. 571–610.

Suddaby, R., 2010, 'Challenges for Institutional Theory', *Journal of Management Inquiry*, 19 (1), pp. 14–20.

Suijs, J., 2005, 'Voluntary Disclosure of Bad News', *Journal of Business Finance & Accounting*, 32 (7–8), pp. 1423–1435.

Sweeney, L. and Coughlan, J., 2008, 'Do Different Industries Report Corporate Social Responsibility Differently? An Investigation through the Lens of Stakeholder Theory', *Journal of Marketing Communications*, 14 (2), pp. 113–124.

Tarca, A., 2004, 'International Convergence of Accounting Practices: Choosing between IAS and US GAAP', *Journal of International Financial Management & Accounting*, 15 (1), pp. 60–91.

Thomas, J. B. and McDaniel Jr, R. R., 1990, 'Interpreting Strategic Issues: Effects of Strategy and the Information-Processing Structure of Top Management Teams', *Academy of Management Journal*, 33 (2), pp. 286–306.

Thompson, J. and Houlder, V., 2012, 'Starbucks Faces Boycott Calls over Tax Affairs', *Financial Times*. Available at www.ft.com/content/5cd14dcc-187f-11e2-8705-00144feabdc0. Accessed 13/01/2019.

Toms, J. S., 2002, 'Firm Resources, Quality Signals and the Determinants of Corporate Environmental Reputation: Some UK Evidence', *The British Accounting Review*, 34 (3), pp. 257–282.

Vanhamme, J. and Grobben, B., 2009, '"Too Good to Be True!": The Effectiveness of CSR History in Countering Negative Publicity', *Journal of Business Ethics*, 85, pp. 273–283.

Verrecchia, R. E., 1983, 'Discretionary Disclosure', *Journal of Accounting and Economics*, 5, pp. 179–194.

Verrecchia, R. E., 2001, 'Essays on Disclosure', *Journal of Accounting and Economics*, 32 (1–3), pp. 97–180.

Vodafone, 'Taxation and Our Total Economic Contribution to Public Finances 2016–17', Available at www.vodafone.com/content/index/about/sustainability/operating-responsibly/tax-and-our-contribution-to-economies.html. Accessed 13/01/2019.

Vollmann, T. E., 1991, 'Cutting the Gordian Knot of Misguided Performance Measurement', *Industrial Management & Data Systems*, 91 (1), pp. 24–26.

Walmart, 2017, 'Global Responsibility Report', Available at https://cdn.corporate.walmart.com/6c/d4/d2a7f2c644c9a696063b083ca932/wmt-2017-grr-report-final.pdf. Accessed 13/01/2019.

Watson, A., Shrives, P. and Marston, C., 2002, 'Voluntary Disclosure of Accounting Ratios in the UK', *The British Accounting Review*, 34 (4), pp. 289–313.

Weick, K. E., 1995, *Sensemaking in organizations* (Vol. 3), Thousand Oaks, SAGE Publications.

Williams, O. F., 2004, 'The UN Global Compact: The Challenge and the Promise', *Business Ethics Quarterly*, 14 (4), pp. 755–774.

Williamson, O. E., 1975, *Markets and hierarchies*, New York, Free Press.

WPP, 'Sustainability Report 2016/17', Available at https://sites.wpp.com/sustainabilityreports/2016/. Accessed 15/01/2019.

4 Current status of tax transparency in CSR reporting

Introduction

Having looked at the legal changes surrounding tax transparency and identified the most relevant theories pertinent to CSR and tax transparency, we now move to our empirical study of tax transparency development over recent years. Our sample covers 30 large listed multinational enterprises in 5 countries (UK, Finland, Germany, France and USA) over the period 2012–2017. We examined how tax transparency was embedded into these enterprises' reporting to stakeholders. Results help gauge how willing the firms are to disclose their tax-related information and whether their tax transparency increased over time. We report statistics on the components of our tax transparency score, cross-country and cross-industry differences, using examples from actual reporting. Additionally, we provide some case studies on how corporations have reacted to tax scandals by using tax transparency reporting.

4.1 Measuring tax transparency

4.1.1 Tax transparency scale

As outlined in Chapter 2, we measure tax transparency on a simple five-point scale for the purposes of our empirical research. The scale includes quantitative as well as qualitative information, as both types are relevant for tax transparency. The purpose of the scale is to measure the overall extent of tax transparency without giving precedence to any one component. Table 4.1 summarises the components of the scale: the sum of corporate income taxes, tax strategy, geographical spread, tax footprint and other information. We assigned each component a value of 1 if it was disclosed or at least mentioned in a stand-alone CSR or integrated report. Our scale does not account for the extensiveness or depth of information provided as it serves as an indicative measure of tax transparency reporting by the firms.

Next, we specify certain matters regarding the logic of assigning scores to the components. Additionally, we provide several examples from the companies' reports, illustrating the type of information provided.

Table 4.1 Tax transparency scale

Component	*Examples*	*Importance*	*Limitations*
1 Sum of corporate income taxes	Current tax expense or effective tax rate during the financial year.	Corporate income taxes are the main focus in the corporate tax debate and legislative initiatives.	The income tax figure alone is not informative if the reader cannot compare it to, for example, profit or revenue. Available in financial statements.
2 Tax strategy	Characterisation of tax strategy or policy, company's stance towards the use of tax havens.	Tax strategy impacts the corporate income taxes (as well as other taxes) paid. Legislative incentives target aggressive strategies and public attention is drawn to revelations of tax planning schemes.	Subjectivity of information given, principles vs. practice.
3 Geographical spread	Income taxes (and other taxes paid) by country or other geographical region (as defined by company).	The tax competition between countries and the fact that most large companies are highly multinational in their operations makes the geographical spread of taxes relevant.	The income tax figure alone is not informative if the reader cannot compare it to, for example, profit or revenue by region.
4 Tax footprint	VAT, payroll taxes, property taxes, etc.	Gives a fuller picture of the tax contribution of a company instead of focusing only on CIT. Incorporates ideas of the total tax contribution.	The distinction should be made between taxes collected on behalf of the government (e.g. VAT or withholding taxes) and taxes actually borne by the company (e.g. non-deductible VAT) to avoid misleading presentation.
5 Other	References to the societal importance of tax payments or the government's tax policy, self-characterisations such as "major taxpayer".	Gives insight into company's view on the importance/relevance of tax in CSR, tax-related risks faced by the company.	Informative value regarding company's actual performance may be low. Subjective.

Income taxes paid

Total current tax expense can be found in the companies' financial statements. Additionally, financial statements prepared in accordance with IFRS (IAS 12) contain a reconciliation of the effective tax rate (ETR). However, in order to gain a point in the category, the figure must be reported separately in the CSR report or CSR section in the integrated report. Many companies provide a GRI index as part of their CSR reporting. Even if a company refers to its annual report in the GRI index under 201–1 or EC1 (without providing the specific figures required in the indicator), this is not taken as adequate for gaining a point in the category. The rationale behind this approach is to distinguish between companies, as gaining a point requires publishing more than legally required information and, in relation to GRI index, more than just ticking a box with a reference to what is legally required.

Tax strategy

Category tax strategy refers to presenting company's tax strategy, tax policy or stance towards the use of tax havens. This category is very diverse and includes much subjective information prone to interpretation. In our scoring exercise, we followed the principle that the report should contain a stand-alone description of the firm's take on its tax strategy or policy. It may include future plans or comments on the tax governance structures associated with tax function in the company. An example of a concise tax strategy description is found in GlaxoSmithKline's Responsible Business Supplement 2017, where the firm addresses its overall approach to tax and then exemplifies its relationships with tax authorities, international tax framework, transfer pricing and tax havens (GlaxoSmithKline, 2017, p. 16). Some firms explain the logic behind using tax havens, pointing to the fluidity of tax haven definitions – in 2018, the EU removed eight countries from the tax haven list. Societe Generale (2017, p. 247) gives concrete information on the group's actions in the field of tax responsibility and transparency – for example, on the closure of operations in countries and territories deemed non-cooperative by France.

Geographical spread

Our definition of geographical spread is not based on CbC requirements since we are interested in any information that the firm voluntarily provides on its tax-related issues in different geographical segments. Often, detailed CbC information can be considered proprietary and commercially confidential (Cockfield & MacArthur, 2015), which is not shared other than when compulsory by law and sent directly to the tax authorities. Firms choose to share detailed CbC information or only disclose tax-related information of the countries with the biggest operating activities. To receive a point in this category, it is enough to share tax figures from any other region in addition to the one the firm is listed in. Firms from extractive industries and financial institutions in the EU are obliged to disclose CbC tax information due to EITI and CRD IV, respectively, but might not include the information in their CSR reporting.

Tax footprint

The category tax footprint illustrates the tax responsibilities firms have in addition to CIT. This constitutes the total tax burden of a firm, including VAT, payroll taxes, environmental, consumption and many other taxes, depending on the firm's field of industry. Several jurisdictions with rather low levels of income tax may impose numerous additional taxes. For example, the Total Tax Contribution Framework developed by PwC lists countries by the number of taxes a firm has to pay: the totals range from 20 different taxes in South Africa to over 97 in Belgium. By providing a full tax footprint, the firm has an opportunity to demonstrate the scale of its contribution to society. Tax footprint information often exemplifies and provides distinctions between taxes borne (i.e. actual cost to the company) and taxes collected on behalf of governments.

Other

The category 'other' includes any other tax-related remarks made – for example, references to the societal importance of tax payments or the impact of a government's tax policy on the company. Although some companies might have more than one remark falling into this category, there are no additional points for this. This is because the informational value in the category is considered generally lower than in the four other categories that provide more factual information. In this category, firms freely express their tax-related position, often highlighting the importance of tax payments for society and their role as "responsible corporate citizens" that pay their fair share of taxes. Additionally, firms may highlight special tax regimes that are unique to the industry they operate in. For instance, Pernod Ricard (2012/2013, p. 79) discusses alcohol taxation, as it is one of the most relevant to their business: "Tax on spirits should not be a victim of discrimination against imports and must not contravene the rules of World Trade Organization (WTO)". Some firms include such items as deferred taxes in the balance sheet explained as part of their tax transparency, so Finnish-listed company Kemira (2017, p. 7) lists ongoing tax appeals in its tax footprint report 2017.

Summary

Apart from the consideration related to the category "other", we do not consider it appropriate to assess any one component to be of higher importance. Hence our scale grants one point for each category. Although this is arguably a simplification given the variance in the information given, we see this as an apt approach since the informational needs or preferences of different stakeholder groups are likely to vary. Therefore, it would not be justified to emphasise one component over the other. Moreover, we do not use grades within each category, as this would require a great deal of judgement for categories 2 and 5. For categories 1, 3 and 4, the 0 or 1 distinction is clear as the information is either given or not. Neither is it necessary to assess the appropriateness of categories a company chooses to use (i.e. geographical level or types of tax), as this is would again involve subjective judgement, as there is no single standard by which companies need abide.

The scale measures the amount of information given to the readers of the report – i.e. transparency in terms of quantity of voluntary disclosure. The scale itself does not measure the quality of information, but we incorporate the variable of external assurance into our research. An increasing number of companies have chosen to publish their CSR information and have it externally verified by one of the Big-4 audit companies or other independent assurance providers. External verification provides overall assurance of the report without taking a separate stance on tax-related information. External assurance is mandatory for the CbC tax information provided by financial institutions that have to abide by the EU Capital Requirements Directive (CRD IV, Directive 2013/36/EU). However, this information does not need to be included in CSR reporting but is published as a separate report.

Furthermore, the different pieces of information given in reporting reflect the company's view of taxation as part of CSR. It can be argued that the more information is given, the more important and relevant the company views taxation in relation to its CSR policy. Following Weick (1995), reporting can be seen in general as a form of sensemaking by which the organisation produces a collective understanding of itself, or in our case, specifically of its relationship to taxation in the context of CSR. Recognising the significance of tax matters for corporate responsibility and determining a general stance or a more specific policy can be seen as a first step for tax transparency.

In sum, our scale incorporates the main focus of international tax debates – namely, CIT (component 1) and companies' tax policies as the response to the debate (component 2). Additionally, the scale reflects the international dimension of MNCs' taxation (component 3) as well as the total tax contribution thinking (component 4). In our view, a multinational corporation's reporting on tax matters is transparent if it gives comprehensive and high-quality information on components 1–4, and we would also characterise such reporting as best practice for all MNCs independent of industry or country. In addition, we use the category 'other', as it enables the inclusion of other industry- or company-specific information that further contributes to tax transparency.

4.1.2 Choice of companies

Our empirical examination includes 150 large listed multinational companies from five different countries (USA, UK, Germany, France and Finland) and from 11 different industries. This enables us to examine the current state of reporting about tax issues between countries as well as across industries. We had originally chosen 30 companies per country, based on 2012 equity market indices.[1]

However, due to mergers, the number of companies had fallen slightly by 2017, the last year of examination. Altogether, the data comprises analysis of 878 reports or 878 firm-year observations for the time period 2012–2017.

The impact of accounting, legal and finance systems on CSR reporting

The countries chosen represent different accounting, legal and finance systems. Accounting practices and financial disclosure have been found to differ across countries. Explanations for this include the nature of business ownership and financing system, colonial inheritance and invasions; taxation, inflation, level of education, age and size of the accountancy profession; stage of economic development; legal systems; culture; history; geography; language; influence of theory; political systems/social climate; religion; and pure accidents (Nobes, 1998, p. 163). However, the impact of only a minority of these has been tested empirically. The most compelling theories explaining the international differences have addressed the impact of institutional factors, including legal, financing and taxation systems (e.g. Zysman, 1983; Nobes, 1998; Lamb, Nobes & Roberts, 1998; Gee, Haller & Nobes, 2010; Kvaal & Nobes, 2010, 2013). Out of our chosen countries, the USA and UK represent equity-based financing systems, while Germany and France represent credit-based systems. Consequently, the legal systems are based on Anglo-Saxon common law vs. continental European code law. During the past few decades, Finland has transitioned from a credit-based system towards an equity-based system. The countries examined fall into either liberal market-based economies (USA and UK) or coordinated market economies (Germany, France and Finland). However, these divisions are not clear-cut, and significant differences may exist within these groupings.

Given the cross-national variation in financial reporting, similar research examining the determinants of non-financial CSR reporting has been conducted. Chen and Bouvain (2009, p. 302) summarise, “A key factor that has been shown to be influential in determining both the nature and extent of nonfinancial disclosure by corporations is the country in which the business is headquartered”. However, the authors find that institutional differences between liberal market economies (coinciding with equity-based, common law Anglo-Saxon accounting system) and coordinated market economies (coinciding with the credit-based, code-law continental European accounting system) do not adequately explain the cross-national variation in non-financial reporting. Kolk, Walhain and van der Wateringen (2001, p. 15) have found that in relation to variation in environmental disclosures, “national societal pressure seems to play a large role (especially in the UK, The Netherlands and Germany)”. Furthermore, reporting is more widespread in industry sectors that have a substantial direct environmental impact (including chemicals, pharmaceuticals, oil and motor vehicles and parts). Financial companies report less often than average. However, the high reporting rate of UK companies as a whole despite the high number of financial companies shows that other factors than industry are influential. Kolk, Walhain and van der Wateringen (2001) suggest that societal attention/pressures, the higher importance of reporting to shareholders (given the equity-based system) or the influence of ethical investment community can explain the national variation in this case.

Similarly, Meek, Roberts and Gray (1995) found an industry effect concerning voluntary non-financial information in general: the oil, chemicals and mining group tends to provide more voluntary non-financial information. They suppose that this industry group is politically more sensitive than others and relate the finding with the political cost arguments. However, they also find a country effect: "The voluntary disclosure of nonfinancial information appears to be a particularly European phenomenon: both British and Continental European MNCs [multinational corporations] provide more of it than American MNCs do" (Meek, Roberts & Gray, 1995, p. 567). This is not in line with what might be expected from a coordinated market economies (continental European) vs. liberal market economies (Anglo-Saxon) split.

Surveys on the determinants of CSR disclosure compare different countries and various types of disclosures, so it is difficult to draw conclusions on the cross-national variation based on their conflicting findings. Only the size phenomenon, whereby large companies report CSR information more often than smaller ones, is found consistently across studies (Meek, Roberts & Gray, 1995, p. 567). Given these earlier findings, we do not develop hypotheses on the cross-national variation based on the legal, financing or accounting systems. In the light of the previous research presented, as well as the CSR theories discussed in Chapter 3, factors related to reputation, legitimacy and stakeholder pressures offer more convincing explanations for variation in CSR reporting in general and similarly in tax reporting in particular. However, we believe that it is appropriate to include countries representing the different characteristics in terms of legal, financial and accounting systems and to consider the possible impact on the reputation, legitimacy and stakeholder factors.

We choose to focus on the largest listed companies in each country that, according to prior research, are most likely to report most extensively. Hence our results should not be influenced by the size factor, as all the companies can be seen to fall into the same category in their countries (despite large differences in absolute revenue/market capitalisation).

4.1.3 Empirical evidence

First, we examine the prevalence of CSR reporting in our sample. Out of the 878 firm-year observations, 92% produced CSR reporting in the form of a separate CSR report, an integrated report or substantial CSR reporting as part of the annual report. We observe a trend of more widespread adoption of CSR-related reporting in the later years. While in 2012, 92% of firms in our sample reported CSR-related information, in 2017, it reached 99%. There are some country-to-country differences: CSR reporting was the most common in France (99% due to Grenelle Act requirements), followed by Germany (93%), Finland (92%), the UK (91%) and the USA (87%). GRI is the most commonly followed standard: 65% of companies in the sample stated that they used it (application method and levels varying).

Next, we further investigate the results of the tax transparency score: its components, trends and variations across time, countries and industries.

Tax transparency development over time

Most companies provide information on at least one item in our tax transparency score. Out of 878 firm-year observations, the tax transparency score was more than zero in 501 observations (57%). Out of 150 firms, 128 (85%) included at least one item of the tax transparency score as part of their CSR reporting in at least one of the years examined. However, the results demonstrate that companies are not generally willing to disclose extensive tax-related information or do not consider it relevant to their CSR reporting. During 2012–2017, all firms disclosed on average 1.3 items as measured on our five-point scale (median equalled 1 and standard deviation 1.5). Figure 4.1 shows the development of the mean value of tax transparency score during 2012–2017 in our sample. A clear positive trend is visible: in 2012, firms reported on average less than one item (0.91 points), while in 2017, the number reached 1.55 items. The trend is also explained by the spread of GRI reporting, whereby non-reporting firms in the later years choose to disclose the basic GRI requirement (tax figure) in their voluntary CSR reporting.

Components of the tax transparency score

We investigate the development of individual components of tax transparency with 878 firm-year observations (see Table 4.2). The maximum value of each score component is 1. Companies disclose information more willingly in the categories "tax figure" and "other". The tax figure (mean value of 0.5) is readily

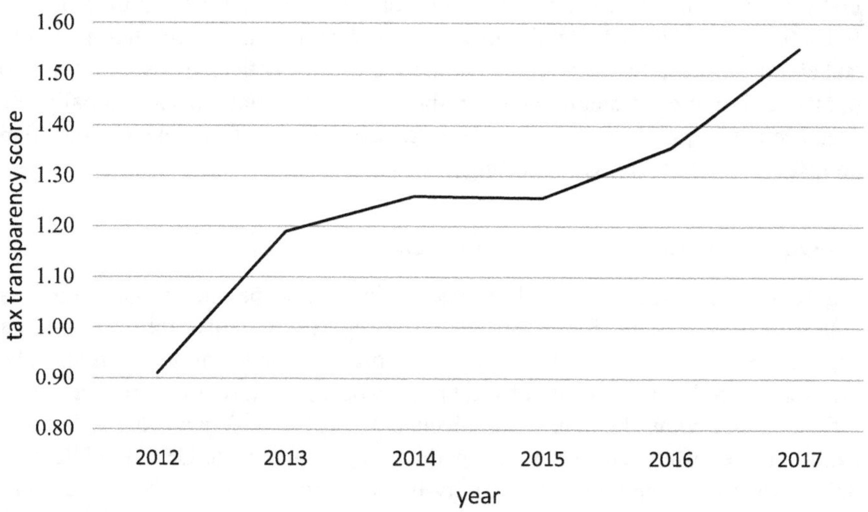

Figure 4.1 Tax transparency score development, 2012–2017

Table 4.2 Descriptive statistics of tax transparency score and its components (n = 878)

Variable	*Mean*	*Median*	*SD*	*Min*	*Max*
Tax figure (CIT)	0.5	0	0.5	0	1
Tax strategy	0.2	0	0.4	0	1
Tax footprint	0.1	0	0.3	0	1
Geographical spread	0.2	0	0.4	0	1
Other	0.4	0	0.5	0	1
Tax transparency score	1.3	1.0	1.5	1	5

available from financial statements and hence its inclusion in the CSR report or CSR section of IR is very straightforward and does not require additional effort. Furthermore, the GRI reporting standards include a tax figure under economic impacts, which makes companies applying the standard likely to report it. In the category “other”, firms freely comment on their tax activities, and we observe that reporting on that category is widespread with a mean value of 0.4 and a standard deviation of 0.5. Tax strategy, tax footprint and geographical spread are the items that few firms choose to disclose in their CSR reporting. Of 150 firms, only 28 firms disclosed some information on their tax footprint and 47 on geographical spread. Tax footprint information is disclosed most often by firms headquartered in Finland (57% of all observations where tax footprint is disclosed), the UK (31%) and France (10%) and by one US company. German companies chose not to disclose this type of information. Regarding geographical spread, disclosure is observable across all countries, but most geographical spread disclosures come from Finland accounting for 63% of disclosures in that category.

We now turn to the components the tax transparency score has developed over time (see Figure 4.2). A positive trend is observed in all components with especially higher growth in tax strategy and “other”. Since the period of examination 2012–2017 coincides with large tax scandals and increased attention from stakeholders, these two categories can be the most practicable way for firms to pursue legitimation strategies and to re-build tainted reputation. Additionally, the requirement to publish a tax strategy established by the UK Finance Act 2016 contributes to the increased reporting in this category.

Cross-country differences in tax transparency

Figure 4.3 illustrates substantial differences in tax transparency reporting across countries. On average, Finnish-listed firms report 2.5 items from our 5-point transparency score, while the US firms report on average only 0.5 items. The differences in the mean value of the tax transparency score are statistically significant. In our view, the liberal capitalism hypothesis (Avi-Yonah, 2014) does not explain these differences in tax transparency reporting, as the USA and UK both belong to liberal capitalism and equity-based financing system but have completely different patterns in tax transparency. Hence cross-country differences are not explained by financing and legal systems. The results are in line with

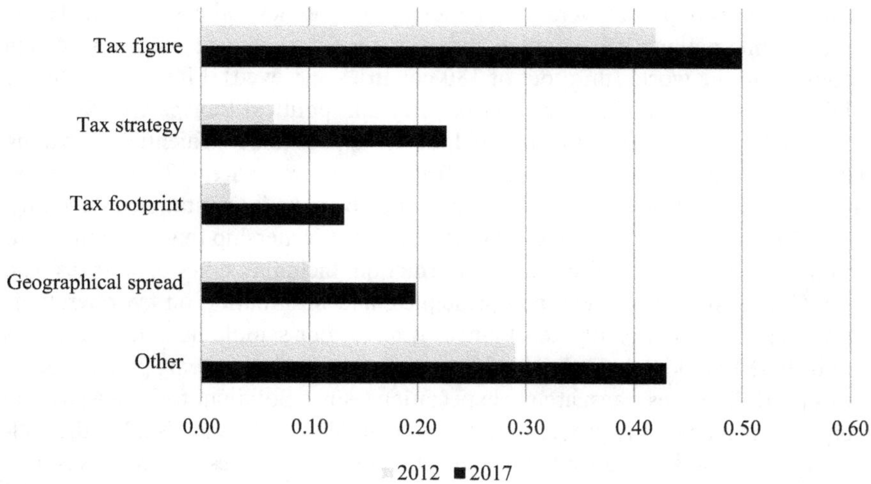

Figure 4.2 Components of tax transparency score in 2012 and 2017

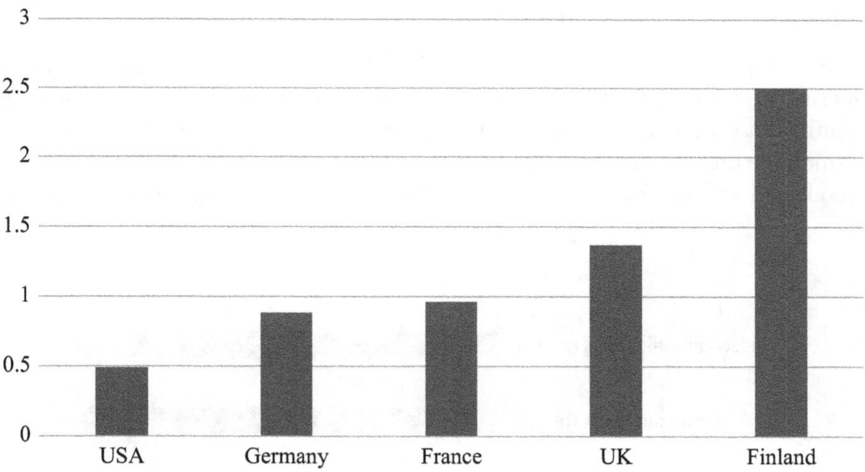

Figure 4.3 Average tax transparency score by country, 2012–2017

Meek, Roberts and Gray's (1995) finding that European MNEs disclose more CSR-related information compared to their US-based counterparts. MNEs based in USA may have a high threshold on what to consider proprietary tax information and prefer not to share it as part of their CSR reporting. Institutional theory and stakeholder theory can be used to explain cross-country differences where institutional settings and different levels of stakeholders' expectations can explain differences, but more research is needed to understand what the country-specific drivers of tax transparency are.

Why is tax transparency so much more pronounced amongst Finnish firms? Finland scores high on several international transparency indices – e.g. in Transparency International's corruption index, it scored as one of the least corrupt countries in the world (third out of 180 countries surveyed). Finland also scores high on economic/institutional transparency and political transparency as compiled by Williams (2015). Institutional factors appear to be influential in shaping tax transparency reporting of Finnish firms, where transparency is perceived as a virtue, a sign of honesty and is strengthened by trust in institutions. Secondly, since 2015, Finnish companies with majority state ownership (e.g. Fortum in our sample) are required to disclose tax information, including taxes paid, taxes paid on a CbC basis, tax strategy and principles, and information on tax operations in tax havens. Additionally, ten Finnish firms in our sample have the state as a minority shareholder through its holding company Solidium. Being part of Solidium's portfolio raises transparency expectations, since Solidium follows a specific corporate responsibility programme as a shareholder. As Finland is a Nordic welfare state, it could be argued that the general public's attitudes towards taxes may be more positive and taxes are more likely viewed as a contribution to funding the general welfare of society.

Tax transparency across industries

The sample consisted of firms from a wide range of industries. Figure 4.4 summarises the tax transparency score across selected industries with statistically significant differences in mean values. Telecommunications and basic materials exhibit the highest tax transparency scores of 2.2 and 2.1, respectively. Consumer goods and services have the lowest tax transparency score with on average only

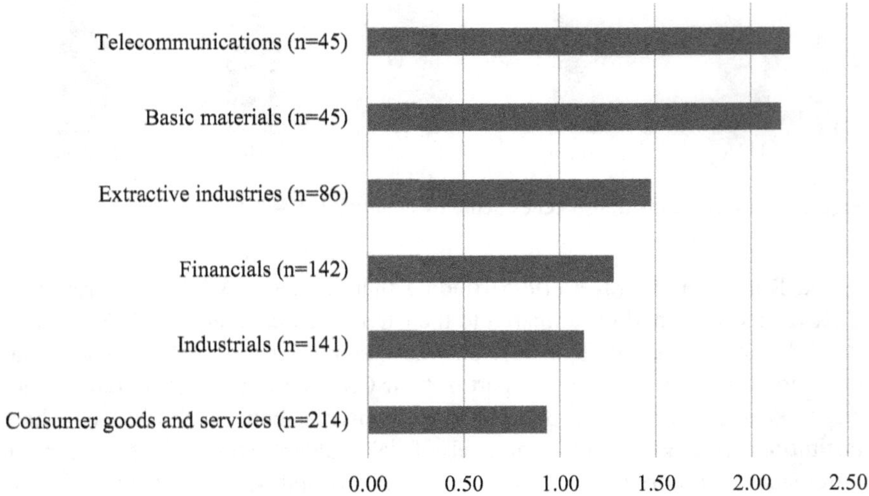

Figure 4.4 Tax transparency score by industry in selected industries, 2012–2017

one item disclosed, while extractive industries and financials disclose on average 1.5 items. The results demonstrate that industries that are subject to industry-specific disclosure requirements (EITI for basic materials and extractive industries and CRD IV for the financial industry in the EU) tend to have higher transparency scores, while unregulated industries disclose a bare minimum of information. The results of this analysis shall be taken with caution since it is affected by the inclusion of the US firms that demonstrate on average very low levels of voluntary tax-related disclosure.

Many MNEs choose to have their CSR reports audited by independent auditors. On average, 59% of firms in our sample had their CSR or equivalent reports assured either fully or partially. While in 2012, this figure was 47%, it rose to 76% in 2017, indicating an increased demand in assured CSR reports as well as a developing market for CSR assurance professionals. Assurance was provided by Big-4 accounting firms for 29% of reports in 2012; in 2017, 53% of the reports were assured by Big-4 accounting firms. These results of CSR assurance are not easily comparable because some firms have chosen only a few indicators to be audited. For instance, French companies have the CSR section required by Grenelle Acts audited but they may also have another separate CSR report which might not be audited (or only partially audited).

4.1.4 Tax transparency after tax scandals

Vodafone

The British telecommunications company Vodafone was one of the companies with the most extensive reporting, scoring a full 5 points on our scale in each year observed. Vodafone has published an extensive separate tax report every year since 2011/12, with certain sections externally assured. This can be viewed as pioneering practice. Vodafone provides the reason for its extensive reporting: "The amount of tax paid by large companies is a matter of significant public debate and scrutiny" (Vodafone, 2011/12, p. 1).

The company experienced public scrutiny in the form of certain major tax disputes. Tax reporting offers an opportunity to give information and present the company's stance in the matter. In the 2011/12 report, Vodafone provided information on the major tax disputes it faced in the UK (concluded in 2010), and a tax claim by Indian tax authorities related to a business acquisition in 2007. However, Vodafone's taxation featured in the headlines more strongly in 2013 after Vodafone sold its stake in the American mobile phone company Verizon. As Grice (2013) reports, based on the existing tax arrangements, the company avoided paying any tax in the UK on the £84 billion profit. Vodafone's Verizon shares were owned by a holding company based in the Netherlands, where the tax rules provided an exemption on capital gains from the sale of shares by Dutch companies. However, the UK had similar exemption rules to those in the Netherlands, meaning the sale would not have been taxable in the UK either. Grice (2013) reports that the UK Treasury came under pressure to review the rules allowing this, as not taxing such windfall profits was viewed as unfair to other UK taxpayers. Consequently, in the 2012/13 report, Vodafone dedicated a section explaining the background of the Verizon sales deal and the basis for the non-taxability. Regarding the purpose of the exemption rules, the section explains that "a number of other EU countries have similar provisions in place, all of which are designed to stimulate long-term corporate investment and consequential broader benefits for the wider economy" (Vodafone, 2012/13, p. 6). Furthermore, the company dedicated a section in the report explaining why it pays little or no UK corporation tax: it points out to significant investments, reliefs granted by UK tax rules and low profits due to the competitive environment in the UK. Additionally, the reporting states that corporation tax, the main focus of the tax avoidance debate, is a small portion of businesses' total tax contribution. In the appendix, Vodafone lists almost 50 different tax types that the operating companies pay globally.

The extensiveness and content of the reporting seems to be well explained through the stakeholder and legitimation/reputation risk management theories. Vodafone recognised that taxation is a significant matter to stakeholders, especially governments, as well as the media and public due to the "public scrutiny" it faced in the tax cases listed previously. Vodafone also seems to be building and maintaining legitimacy through explaining the reasons behind its low CIT in the UK and listing other ways (i.e. other taxes and payments to governments and investments) it contributes to public finances and infrastructure. Furthermore, Vodafone appeals to the company's legal obligation to act in the interest of shareholders, which also include, for example, pension investment funds profiting a wider public. These comments can also be assessed from the reputation risk management perspective, particularly as Vodafone sells services to consumers. Damage to reputation due to perceived irresponsible tax behaviour could potentially lead to an adverse impact on sales. In terms of Benoit's image restoration strategies, we could find examples of bolstering (drawing attention to other taxes paid) and transcendence (redefining the context and providing rationale in terms of responsibility to shareholders). This would correspond to Lindblom's legitimation strategy 3, whereby the organisation tries to identify its output with the public perception of what is appropriate. Apart from legitimacy, stakeholder and reputation management theories, Vodafone's example is a demonstration of signalling theory when the firm releases information that would not be available for its stakeholders under normal circumstances.

Starbucks

After Starbucks was caught up in a tax scandal in the UK in 2012, described in Chapter 1, there was no change in its global responsibility reporting regarding tax. Starbucks does not include tax in any of its global responsibility reports from 2012 to 2017, except for a reference to annual reports in a separate 2012 GRI index. It is important to note that the tax-related publicity was focused on UK taxes, whereas the company is headquartered in the USA and compiles its responsibility reports on a global level. As we noted earlier, tax-related matters are rarely reported in the USA in comparison to the UK. However, in 2014, Starbucks yielded to public criticism and changed its tax policy in the UK. This was reported in the UK media, most likely reaching a wider public than separate CSR reporting would have done. Hence it seems fair to conclude that additional tax-related responsibility reporting was perhaps not deemed necessary for the purposes of reputation risk management and (re-)building legitimacy. This would explain the absence of tax-related information in Starbucks' reporting despite the media attention to the matter.

Nordea

The financial group Nordea suffered hits to its reputation due to the information leaked in Panama Papers in 2016. It was revealed that Nordea's unit in Luxembourg had founded almost 400 companies in tax haven jurisdictions in Panama and the British Virgin Islands for its wealthy private clients (Knus-Galán, 2016). Owning a company in a tax haven is not illegal unless the information is not disclosed to the tax authorities of the owner's home country. Nordea has admitted that before 2009, it did not check if its clients used the bank's services for the purpose of evading taxes (Knus-Galán, 2016). In the aftermath of the Panama Papers in 2017, the Luxembourg financial supervisory authority (CSSF) charged Nordea S.A. and eight other financial institutions fines for non-compliance with the money laundering regulation in Luxembourg (CSSF, 2017). The Swedish financial supervisory authority on the other hand did not punish Nordea for the revelations in the Panama Papers as an inspection showed that Nordea had already been charged fines for the same violations of money laundering regulation discovered in 2015 (Toivonen, 2017).

Nordea makes direct references to the Panama Papers in its 2016 responsibility reporting, for example in a section titled "Earnings Trust from Customers and Society":

> During the year, Nordea has encountered incidents that bruised our customers' trust in us. In April, Nordea was pointed out as one of several actors in the 'Panama Papers', where the media portrayed financial advice given regarding tax structures as unethical. [. . .] We understand that the public perception of compliance goes beyond regulatory requirements, and re-strengthening customer trust is our very top priority.
>
> (Nordea, 2016, p. 5)

Nordea insists it has taken the revelations and the strong public reaction seriously. It concludes that its internal investigation "found no evidence that employees initiated the establishment of offshore structures, or actively contributed to customers' potential tax evasion" (Nordea, 2016, p. 12). However, as the media portrayed financial tax-related advice given by Nordea as unethical, Nordea recognised that ethical expectations from its stakeholders go beyond legal requirements. It is important to note that the public attention in this case was directed to Nordea's practice of advising its customers, not to the governance of its own taxes. As a response to public attention, Nordea observed that it had established a tax policy on customer advice in 2016, which contains for example the following principles: "Nordea pays attention to its customers' reputational risks and does not encourage or facilitate tax schemes of its customers that are regarded as tax evasion" and "Nordea does not encourage or facilitate tax schemes of its customers that may be legal but perceived as aggressive tax planning or not in line with Nordea's internal ethical standards" (Nordea, 2016, p. 12). Furthermore, in its materiality analysis, Nordea identifies transparent tax management as a base issue that must be addressed to reach an elementary level. The media and social media are identified as stakeholders for which tax is a priority.

Again, the themes familiar from legitimation, reputation risk management and stakeholder theories seem to provide insights on the reasons behind Nordea's reporting. Nordea aimed to legitimise itself as a responsible actor that has not broken the law but recognises that it needed to go a step further in order to comply with ethical expectations from stakeholders. This is also important for mending the financial group's reputation that suffered from the revelations. It seems that the reporting includes the use of Benoit's corrective action and mortification strategies, as Nordea acknowledges responsibility and reports how it has improved its processes. This corresponds to Lindblom's legitimation strategy 1, communicating changes in organisation's conduct that have been made in response to public's expectations. Although the Finnish social democratic party (SDP) decided to end its customer relationship with Nordea, at least in part due to the Panama Papers (Koivuranta, 2016), it is unlikely that the financial group suffered significant financial impact due to customer boycotts.

Summary

Tax transparency is not a concept set in stone and includes many nuanced components. In our simple five-point scale, we attempt to capture a firm's income tax payments, tax strategy, tax footprint, geographical spread of taxes and any other tax-related information that the firm is willing to disclose. While tax transparency is still an emerging phenomenon, we observe a steady growth in the amount of tax-related information MNEs are voluntarily providing in their CSR reporting. The most commonly reported items are income tax figure and tax strategy, while tax footprint and the geographical spread of taxes are the least often disclosed. Cross-country differences demonstrate that MNEs from some countries (e.g. Finland and the UK) are more tax transparent due to institutional factors and different levels of stakeholder expectations. Examples of reporting after-tax scandals demonstrate how firms utilise tax transparency reporting in order to re-build reputation and legitimise their actions. Tax transparency requires effort and a substantial amount of planning in order to provide meaningful information where quality of disclosures should drive the process. Best practices and future developments in tax reporting are the focus of the next chapter.

Note

1 Companies in Dow Jones 30 Index for USA, FTSE 30 Index for UK, DAX 30 Index for Germany, 30 randomly chosen companies from the CAC 40 Index for France and 30 largest companies in Finland (the 25 OMX 25 Index companies and the five next largest measured in market capitalisation).

References

Avi-Yonah, R. S., 2014, 'Corporate Taxation and Corporate Social Responsibility', *New York University Journal of Law & Business*, 11 (1), pp. 1–29.

Chen, S. and Bouvain, P., 2009, 'Is Corporate Responsibility Converging? A Comparison of Corporate Responsibility Reporting in the USA, UK, Australia and Germany', *Journal of Business Ethics*, 87, pp. 299–317.

Cockfield, Arthur J., and Carl D. MacArthur, 2015, 'Country-by-Country Reporting and Commercial Confidentiality', *Canadian Tax Journal/Revue Fiscale Canadienne*, 63 (3), 627–660.

CSSF, 'Commission de Surveillance du Secteur Financier, 2017', Press Release 17/44. Panama Papers: Results of the CSSF's Analysis and Subsequent Enforcement Procedures. Available at www.cssf.lu/fileadmin/files/Publications/Communiques/Communiques_2017/PR1744_panama_papers_201217.pdf. Accessed 31/05/2019.

Gee, M., Haller, A. and Nobes, C., 2010, 'The Influence of Tax on IFRS Consolidated Statements: The Convergence of Germany and the UK', *Accounting in Europe*, 7 (1), pp. 97–122.

GlaxoSmithKline plc (GSK), 'Responsible Business Supplement 2017', Available at https://www.gsk.com/media/4756/responsible-business-supplement-2017.pdf. Accessed 05/07/2018.

Grice, A., 2013, 'Vodafone's £84bn tax avoidance bonanza: Nothing for taxpayers in Verizon deal while bankers share £500m in fees', The Independent. Available at https://www.independent.co.uk/news/business/news/vodafones-84bn-tax-avoidance-bonanza-nothing-for-taxpayers-in-verizon-deal-while-bankers-share-500m-8794169.html. Accessed 25/11/2017.

Kemira, 2017, 'Tax Footprint', Available at https://media.kemira.com/kemiradata/2018/03/2017-kemira-tax-footprint-report.pdf. Accessed 15/04/2019.

Knus-Galán, M., 2016, 'Nordea perustanut asiakkailleen satoja yhtiöitä veroparatiiseihin', *MOT Yleisradio*. Available at https://yle.fi/aihe/artikkeli/2016/04/03/nordea-perustanut-asiakkailleen-satoja-yhtioita-veroparatiiseihin. Accessed 06/01/2019.

Koivuranta, E., 2016, 'Nordea-kohu jatkuu: SDP vaihtaa pankkia', *Yleisradio*. Available at https://yle.fi/uutiset/3-8811110. Accessed 06/01/2019.

Kolk, A., Walhain, S. and van der Wateringen, S., 2001, 'Environmental Reporting by the Fortune Global 250: Exploring the Influence of Nationality and Sector', *Business Strategy and the Environment*, 10, pp. 15–28.

Kvaal, E. and Nobes, C., 2010, 'International Differences in IFRS Policy Choice: A Research Note', *Accounting and Business Research*, 40 (2), pp. 173–187.

Kvaal, E. and Nobes, C., 2013, 'International Variations in Tax Disclosures', *Accounting in Europe*, 10 (2), pp. 241–273.

Lamb, M., Nobes, C. and Roberts, A., 1998, 'International Variations in the Connections between Tax and Financial Reporting', *Accounting and Business Research*, 28 (3), pp. 173–188.

Meek, G., Roberts, C. and Gray, S., 1995, 'Factors Influencing Voluntary Annual Report Disclosures by U.S., U.K. and Continental European Multinational Corporations', *Journal of International Business Studies*, 26 (3), pp. 555–572.

Nobes, C., 1998, 'Towards a General Model of the Reasons for International Differences in Financial Reporting', *Abacus*, 34 (2), pp. 162–187.

Nordea, 'Sustainability Report 2016', Available at www.nordea.com/Images/33-169617/Nordea_Sustainability_Report_2016.pdf. Accessed 31/05/2019.

Pernod Ricard, 'Registration Document 2012/2013', Available at www.pernod-ricard.com/en/download/file/fid/7985/. Accessed 09/07/2019.

Societe Generale, '2017 Registration Document, Annual Financial Report 2016', Available at www.societegenerale.com/sites/default/files/documents/Document%20de%20r%C3%A9f%C3%A9rence/2017/Societe-Generale-DDR-2017-15032017-ENG.pdf. Accessed 11/08/2018.

Toivonen, T., 2017, 'Kahden ruotsalaispankin veroparatiisitutkintaa jatketaan – Nordealle ja Handelsbankenille ei lisärapsuja', *Yleisradio*. Available at https://yle.fi/uutiset/3-9517574. Accessed 06/01/2019.

Vodafone, 'Tax and Our Total Contribution to Public Finances 2011/12', Available at www.vodafone.com/content/dam/sustainability/2016/tax_report/vodafone-tax-report-2012.pdf. Accessed 31/05/2019.

Vodafone, 'Tax and Our Total Contribution to Public Finances 2012/13', Available at www.vodafone.com/content/dam/vodafone-images/sustainability/downloads/vodafone_2013_tax.pdf. Accessed 31/05/2019.

Weick, K. E., 1995, *Sensemaking in organizations*, Thousand Oaks, SAGE Publications.

Williams, A., 2015, 'A Global Index of Information Transparency and Accountability', *Journal of Comparative Economics*, 43 (3), pp. 804–824.

Zysman, J., 1983, *Government, markets and growth: Financial systems and the politics of industrial change*, Ithaca, Cornell University Press.

5 Future of tax transparency

Introduction

In this chapter, we outline various possible future developments related to tax transparency. We introduce and assess the most recent developments in advancing tax transparency: both mandatory and voluntary reporting initiatives as well as best practices already adopted by companies. These provide guidelines and benchmarks for individual companies seeking to comply with new official and unofficial reporting demands as well as improving their existing reporting. We provide a framework for evaluating the quality of information reported and emphasise that the usefulness of information should be the future focus in tax transparency rather than simply demanding larger quantities of data. We note the cost constraints to increased reporting, as well as limits to information processing capabilities, and introduce how AI can assist in overcoming these hurdles. Finally, we summarise our view on tax transparency as part of the wider CSR framework pinpointing avenues for future research.

5.1 The role of CSR standards in changing tax transparency

In Chapter 1, we provided an overview of changing legislation related to tax transparency and identified voluntary standards and guidelines that contain tax transparency references. Of all CSR standards, GRI is one of the most widely used around the world. GRI standards are developed through a transparent, multi-stakeholder process through the GRI's independent standard-setting body, namely Global Sustainability Standards Board (GSSB).

In 2017, GSSB started a project on tax and payments to governments with the aim to develop new, specific disclosures related to tax and to promote greater transparency on reporting organisation approaches to taxes. Like other GRI standards, this new standard would be followed by an organisation in the future if taxation is identified as a material topic in the organisation's materiality assessment, meaning that it recognised as sufficiently important that it is essential to report on it. From January 2018, a specific multi-stakeholder Technical Committee worked to develop a draft of GRI Tax and Payments to Governments Standard, which was opened for public consultation in Spring 2019. According to

GRI, stakeholder feedback is critical in standards development. The standard is expected to be released in final form at the end of 2019. Further, we elaborate on the elements of the draft of Tax and Payments to Governments Standard.

As of winter 2018/19, the draft contains five blocks of disclosure (see Figure 5.1).

Disclosures in the draft standard are divided into two types of disclosure: management approach and topic-specific disclosures. Management disclosures include three blocks: (1) approach to tax and payments to governments; (2) tax governance, control and risk management; tax governance, control and risk management; and (3) stakeholder engagement and management of concerns related to tax and payments. Topic-specific disclosures relate to entities and activities by tax jurisdiction and CbC reporting.

We examine each of the disclosures and evaluate each item in light of changing regulations and theories discussed in Chapter 3.

Disclosure 1 – Approach to tax and payments to governments currently includes the following:

1 whether the organisation has a tax strategy and, if so, a link to this strategy if publicly available;
2 the governance body or executive-level position within the organisation that formally reviews and approves the tax strategy and the frequency of this review;
3 the approach to regulatory compliance described in the tax strategy; and
4 how the tax strategy is linked to the business and sustainable development strategies of the organisation and to the broader economic needs of the countries in which the organisation operates.

This disclosure corresponds to our transparency score on tax policy/strategy but provides more structure and items that should be considered for disclosure. Availability of tax strategy may signal a company's overall approach to taxes. One may

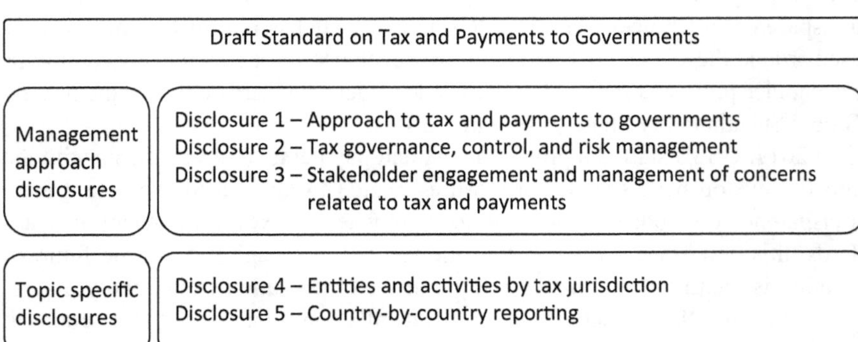

Figure 5.1 Disclosures in GRI draft Standard on Tax and Payments to Governments

Source: GRI

observe the influence of changing institutional setting, whereby EU and OECD-led tax transparency initiatives penetrate the field of voluntary CSR reporting. An attempt is made to link tax strategy to the broader economic need of the countries in which the organisation operates. As discussed in Chapter 3, descriptive qualitative disclosures related to tax transparency can be used by companies for legitimising and reputation management purposes.

Disclosure 2 – Tax governance, control and risk management including the following:

1 A description of the tax governance and control framework, including

  a the governance body or executive-level position within the organisation accountable for compliance with tax strategy;
  b how the stated approach to tax and payments to governments or tax strategy is embedded within the organisation;
  c the approach to tax risks, including how risks are identified, managed and monitored; and
  d how compliance with the tax governance and control framework is evaluated.

2 A description of the mechanisms for reporting concerns about unethical or unlawful behaviour and the organisation's integrity in relation to taxes.
3 A description of the assurance process for disclosures on tax and payments to governments, including, if applicable, a reference to the assurance report, statement or opinion.

The purpose of Disclosure 2 could serve legitimising purposes by sharing information on the internal tax governance structure. Much attention is paid to internal governance structures that oversee, monitor and evaluate tax-related issues. Potentially, information on internal structures and mechanisms for reporting concerns about unethical or unlawful behaviour could be considered to be of a proprietary nature and hence remain undisclosed. Assurance process for disclosures on tax and payments to governments is included as one of the disclosure points. Assurance mechanism are important and CSR reports have long been assured against GRI compliance. However, introducing a new assurance element will require that the assurance industry develops skills and capabilities to meet this requirement.

Disclosure 3 – Stakeholder engagement and management of concerns related to tax and payments

1 A description of the approach to stakeholder engagement and management of stakeholder concerns related to tax and payments to governments, including the following:

  a the approach to engagement with tax authorities;
  b the approach to public policy advocacy on tax and payments to governments; and

c processes for collecting and considering the views and concerns of external stakeholders.

Disclosure 3 underlines the importance of stakeholder engagement and collecting information from company stakeholders. Like CSR reporting in general, having strong roots in identifying and prioritising stakeholders, tax-related disclosures are envisioned to have the same features. Potential conflicts of interests arise when stakeholders identified as core for the main firm activities are not the same as for the purpose of the tax disclosures. We may expect to see conflicting narratives on meeting profit maximisation vs. paying a transparent and fair amount of taxes. Collecting data from stakeholders, such as, textile workers in third countries that are in a locked-in position where their livelihood depends on the job from the firm in question may be problematic. Similarly, engaging in stakeholder dialogue with tax authorities and stakeholders in countries tainted by corruption may turn into window dressing exercises without meaningful implications for the level of tax transparency.

Disclosures 4 and 5 relate more specifically to numerical information of a tax-related nature.

Disclosure 4 – Entities and activities by tax jurisdiction, including the following:

1 A list of all tax jurisdictions where the entities included in the organisation's audited financial statements, or in the financial information filed on public record, are resident for tax purposes.
2 For each tax jurisdiction in which the organisation has resident entities, as listed in Disclosure 4-a:

 a the number of entities;
 b the names of the principal entities;
 c the primary activities of the entities; and
 d the number of employees (should report the following additional information: total employee remuneration for each tax jurisdiction in which the organisation has resident entities).

Information mentioned in Disclosure 4 is useful for identifying the operational structure of the firm because it would potentially disclose which entities are created for investment purposes only. Currently, companies have to disclose information on its operating segments according to IFRS 8 Operating Segments that sets criteria for reporting segments based on their operational size or amount of assets tied in them.[1] Proposed Disclosure 4 in turn, if applied, would offer a geographical view of the entities included in the corporation structure. This information would be useful for identifying if the firm has any entities listed in the EU tax heaven list or if it has engaged in establishing entities likely serving tax avoidance motives. The number of employees and total employee remuneration for each tax jurisdiction in which the organisation has resident entities would potentially shed light on the extent of physical presence and the real activities of the company. A possible challenge associated with this lies in the digitalisation of society where workers are replaced by – e.g. chatbots[2] – so the number of workers does not necessarily translate into the measure of activity in a given jurisdiction.

Disclosure 5 – CbC reporting, for each tax jurisdiction in which the organisation has resident entities as disclosed according to Disclosure 4 the reporting organisation shall report the following information:

1 Revenues by

   a third-party sales; and
   b intra-group transactions of the tax jurisdiction with other tax jurisdictions.

2 Profit/loss before tax.
3 Tangible assets other than cash and cash equivalents.
4 Corporate tax paid on a cash basis.
5 Corporate tax accrued on profit/loss.
6 Reasons for the difference between corporate tax accrued on profit/loss and the tax due if the statutory tax rate is applied to profit/loss before tax.
7 Significant tax incentives.

Moreover, in accordance with Disclosure 5 reporting recommendations, the company should report the following additional information for each of the organisation's listed tax jurisdictions:

a Taxes withheld and paid on behalf of employees;
b Taxes collected from customers on behalf of a tax authority;
c Industry-related and other taxes or payments to governments;
d Significant uncertain tax positions; and
e Balance of intra-company debt held by entities in a tax jurisdiction and the average interest rate paid on that debt.

Disclosure 5 aims to provide meaningful tax transparency by requiring companies to disclose detailed financial statement information that is pertinent to tax. Hence tax transparency is linked to financial reporting and follows the logic of IFRS 8. Since proposed CbC disclosures are rather detailed, a company may refer to regulatory compliance with OECD BEPS and produce a statement that disclosure to the public is not required by law. Our analysis of tax transparency by companies included in our sample demonstrates that some companies refer to the principle of confidentiality, hence declare that disclosure of CbC reporting is linked to proprietary costs. Furthermore, Disclosure 5 relates to tax footprint element in our tax transparency score. Moreover, Disclosure 5 aims to capture disclosure of other tax contributions apart from income tax, such as industry-related and other taxes or payments to governments.

It is important to emphasise that GRI's draft of Tax and Payment to Governments Standard will be released as a standard in the end of 2019 after comments received during stakeholder consultation process are reviewed. Therefore, our discussion of the standard draft serves illustrative purpose in order to compare it with our tax transparency score presented in Chapter 4.

5.2 Designing tax transparency and best practices

5.2.1 Quality characteristics

Reporting publicly about tax-related matters (including the disclosure of quantitative data) can significantly contribute to tax transparency, but only if the reporting is deemed relevant and of high quality by users. The quality characteristics for financial reporting can also be applied to tax-related reporting. The IFRS Conceptual Framework for Financial Reporting (IFRS Foundation, 2018) determines the fundamental characteristics it has to fulfil in order to be useful – i.e. relevance (materiality) and faithful representation (prudence). Enhancing qualitative characteristics are comparability, verifiability, timeliness and understandability. It is important to note that relevance and faithful representation are primary concerns. Even if the information reported may be understandable, verifiable and timely, it would not be useful if it was not relevant. Additionally, the framework considers the cost constraint on useful financial reporting, stating that "the benefit of providing the information needs to justify the cost of providing and using the information" (IFRS Foundation, 2018, p. 6). Similar considerations have been brought forward by the GRI for defining CSR reporting content and quality. The reporting principles for defining content set in GRI-101 are stakeholder inclusiveness, sustainability context, materiality and completeness. Reporting principles for defining report quality are accuracy, balance, clarity, comparability, reliability and timeliness (GRI, 2016, p. 7). The EU defines six key principles for good non-financial reporting: material; fair, balanced and understandable; comprehensive but concise; strategic and forward-looking; stakeholder oriented; and consistent and coherent (European Commission, 2019, p. 5). These characteristics have been summarised and grouped together in Table 5.1. We next look at these characteristics one by one in the context of CSR reporting and tax reporting in particular and suggest how they can guide best practices in tax reporting.

Reporting content: relevance

Relevance in financial reporting means that the information reported affects the decisions made by the users of the information. As such, it has either predictive or confirmatory value, or both (IFRS Foundation, 2018). The crucial concept of materiality is relevance brought to the entity-specific report level (Deloitte, 2018). In CSR reporting, the concept is similar. However, it is concerned with a wider range of impacts and stakeholders (GRI, 2016, p. 10). Relevant topics "can reasonably be considered important for reflecting the organization's economic, environmental, and social impacts, or influencing the decisions of stakeholders" (GRI, 2016, p. 10). Considerations of materiality define which topics are sufficiently important that they need to be reported on. It is also noted in GRI-101 that not

Table 5.1 Quality characteristics of financial and non-financial reporting in different standards/frameworks

Aspect	*IFRS conceptual framework for financial reporting*	*GRI reporting principles (GRI-101)*	*EU key principles for non-financial reporting*
Reporting content	Relevance (materiality)	The four reporting principles for defining content: stakeholder inclusiveness, sustainability context, materiality and completeness	Material Stakeholder oriented
Quality of information	Faithful representation (prudence) Comparability Verifiability	Balance Accuracy Comparability Reliability	*Fair, balanced* and understandable Consistent and coherent *Comprehensive* but concise Strategic and forward-looking
Presentation	Understandability	Clarity	Comprehensive but *concise* Fair, balanced and *understandable*
Timing of reporting	Timeliness	Timeliness	The EU key principles do not specifically mention timeliness (or equivalent)

all material topics are equally important; hence, the emphasis in the report should reflect the relative priority. Defining materiality in CSR reporting requires consideration of a combination of external and internal factors – for instance, the organisation's mission and strategy, broad societal expectations and expectations expressed in international standards and agreements, organisation's influence on other upstream or downstream entities as well as the concerns expressed directly by stakeholders. This is defined through establishing a process for stakeholder engagement by which stakeholders are identified and information on their expectations, interests and information needs is gathered.

In Chapter 3, in relation to stakeholder theory, we touched on the stakeholder dimension of materiality and noted the increased demand for tax-related information from various stakeholder groups – for instance, due to the increased media exposure of MNEs' tax practices and intergovernmental initiatives to counter aggressive tax avoidance. Given that the economic impact of taxes is crucial for funding the functioning of societies and that all corporations are subject to various taxes, it is hard to deny the materiality of the topic. Some MNEs may have smaller corporate tax footprints due to low profits globally or in certain countries, and hence it could be argued that, in this respect, their impact is small. However, in these cases, providing the information and reasonably showing that profits are not artificially transferred to tax havens would be relevant information to many stakeholders.

In companies' CSR reporting, the materiality matrix as recommended by GRI is most often used to display the relative importance of topics that guides reporting. Tax matters can be their own topic, or they may have been grouped under – e.g. economic responsibility. Examples of tax-specific labels include "taxes" (Intel Corporation, 2017–2018), "corporate tax" (Reckitt Benckiser Group plc, 2017), "tax and economic contribution" (GSK, 2016), "indirect economic impact & tax" (Deutsche Post, 2017), "good corporate citizenship and tax contribution" (Neste, 2016), "tax transparency" (Diageo, 2015), "transparent tax management" (Nordea Bank AB, 2017) and "tax policy" (WPP, 2017). All these companies have identified tax matters as material topics in their stakeholder engagement process and so provide at least some information on the topic in their reporting: their scores on our tax transparency scale range from 1 to 5. In general, in all cases, the score based on our scale may not reflect the relative importance granted to topic in the materiality matrix as companies may not be aware of all different aspects of tax reporting (e.g. considering only total group CIT paid and not CbC data, tax footprint or strategy). A few companies have also included the priorities raised by individual stakeholder group. For example, Nordea indicates that "transparent tax management" is a material topic to media and social media (Nordea Bank AB, 2016).

Quality of information: faithful representation

In the IFRS Conceptual Framework, faithful representation means that information is complete, neutral and free from error to the maximum extent possible (IFRS Foundation, 2018). It is easier to apply the concept to CSR reporting by breaking it into the three parts: complete, neutral and free from error.

In the context of CSR reporting, as defined by GRI-101, completeness would require that a report covers all material topics and their boundaries, reflects significant economic, environmental and social impacts and enables stakeholders to assess the organisation's performance in the reporting period. With respect to boundaries, it should be clearly presented if the information reported covers the whole group (including parent and all subsidiaries) or if some parts have been left out and the reasons for and impact of this. This is particularly relevant in the case of CbC reporting: leaving out possible subsidiaries in tax havens would be a severe omission although the impact of tax paid in the local society would be small due to minimal tax rates and hence minimal taxes. Additionally, to enable stakeholders to better assess the significant impacts and the organisation's performance, not only should taxes by country be shown but also revenue, profit, salaries and/or employee numbers. The inclusion of this information would provide a point of comparison between countries and could possibly give indication if aggressive tax avoidance strategies are being employed. If there are any exceptional circumstances justified by a solid business reasons, the reporting organisation could give additional information explaining, for example, exceptionally low profits and hence counter suspicions of tax avoidance.

Neutrality is supported by the exercise of prudence – i.e. caution when making judgements under conditions of uncertainty. In CSR reporting, emissions calculations in different scopes, for instance, require making assumptions as certain information is often not fully available. However, in quantitative information related to taxation, there should be considerably less judgement involved, as different tax figures can be traced to official financial records. However, qualitative information and different types of claims about tax strategy or, for example, the company's role as a "significant tax payer" would need to be evaluated based on the principle of prudence. A large firm may be a significant tax payer compared to smaller firms, but is it so in comparison to its peers and in terms of which taxes?

The third component, free from error, is relatively self-explanatory. We next look at the related concepts of reliability, accuracy and verifiability and how they apply to producing information that is free from error.

Quality of information: reliability, accuracy, verifiability

In financial reporting, the reporting organisation has various reporting processes in place for producing financial information which usually include several control points (automated and/or manual, preventative and corrective). In the context of tax reporting, establishing effective processes for group-wide information gathering from official financial records, with adequate controls in place, would be similarly crucial for the information to be reliable, accurate and verifiable. As previously noted, quantitative tax information is much easier to collect compared to emissions data, for instance, as the figures can be traced from financial records, either in the financial statements (e.g. CIT accrued) or from subledgers (e.g. employee withholding taxes from payroll). In the case of CIT, the company needs to assess if it reports taxes accrued (with or without deferred taxes) or taxes paid (cash movements). This choice should naturally be clearly stated in the report and applied consistently. The new GRI topic-specific standard taxes and payments to government guides reporting towards both taxes accrued and taxes paid. Qualitative information, for example, on tax strategy requires involvement by those charged with management and governance if the reporting organisation does not have a stated policy. Claims about strategy would need to be substantiated with clear approval and commitment from the top, as well as by actual practices, the inclusion of stated policies in firm-wide code-of-conduct and/or other supporting evidence. The group's transfer pricing documentation can also be a point of reference for both quantitative and qualitative information.

Having a clear process and documentation of the information collection, production and calculation also makes verification, either internal or external, possible. Particularly, independent, external verification by professionals specialising in the field works as an additional check for achieving reporting that is free from material error, but also for ensuring completeness, and that prudence has been adequately applied. We return to external assurance later.

Quality of information: balance

According to GRI-101, balanced information "shall reflect positive and negative aspects of the reporting organisation's performance to enable a reasoned assessment of overall performance" (GRI, 2016, p. 13). In practice, the report must avoid selections, omissions or presentation formats that may be likely to influence the user's judgement. In the context of tax reporting, this would mean, for example, responding to negative news, such as revelations of aggressive tax avoidance practices, by offering information on the firm's tax strategy, actual performance and, if relevant, possible corrective measures taken. Nordea and Vodafone offer examples of directly addressing negative publicity, as presented in Chapter 4. Additionally, if the information on year-to-year performance was to show a negative trend, the comparative figures should not be omitted, as this would cause imbalance; rather, the reasons behind the changes should be explained.

Quality of information: comparability

According to GRI (2016, p. 14), comparability refers to (1) presenting changes in the organisation's performance over time and (2) supporting analysis relative to other organisations. Firstly, comparisons over time require that the organisation reports the same indicators yearly and compiles the information supporting them consistently. If calculations are required, formulae and assumptions would need to be used consistently. This should be noted inside organisations when group-wide information is collected. It is important that data collected is clearly defined so that different countries and subsidies report comparable data so that group-wide CbC reporting does not become distorted.

Secondly, for stakeholders to be able to make meaningful comparisons, all enterprises would need to report the same indicators calculated in the same manner, as is the case in financial reporting with international reporting standards (IFRS). GRI and other CSR reporting standards facilitate comparability in the sphere of responsibility reporting. In voluntary tax reporting, GRI has offered most guidelines, but so far, companies have chosen to disclose quantitative and qualitative information rather differently. For instance, geographical spread varies from split to "home and overseas" to regions inside countries, although the most common practice is CbC reporting as recommended by GRI. This is also the most logical level given OECD CbC-reporting requirements to tax authorities and facilitates the most useful comparisons. Even the most common indicator often titled "taxes paid" may be defined differently by different organisations. There is often no specification if this includes only CIT or possibly some other taxes as well or if the figure reported is the accrued sum or taxes actually paid during the year. Tax footprint may include both taxes borne and collected, but there is no clarity for how, for example, employee-related taxes are defined by different organisations.

An additional consideration for comparability would be providing, for example profit, revenue, purchases, salaries and personnel costs per country to facilitate understanding of the reasonability of related tax footprint figures, such as CIT, VAT collected and deducted, employee withholding tax collected and other payroll taxes. The new GRI draft topic-specific standard Tax and Payments to Governments and the EU proposed directive on public CbC tax reporting address this consideration.

Quality of information: strategic and forward-looking

By strategic and forward-looking, the EU guidelines mean that non-financial information should "provide insights into a company's business model, strategy and its implementation, and explain the short, medium, and long-term implications of the information reported" (European Commission, 2017, p. 8). This includes disclosing targets, benchmarks and commitments in quantitative and qualitative terms in order to help stakeholders to put the firm's performance in context and assess future prospects.

As for tax reporting, this aspect is most relevant in relation to tax strategy/policy pursued by the company. Reporting should contain information if aggressive tax arrangements cause risks of arguments with tax authorities and potential re-assessments or possible negative impacts to reputation, for instance. Setting quantitative targets or benchmarks for taxes, however, is not relevant as such since the level of taxes borne and collected depend on other measures (e.g. profitability, revenue and purchases, salaries). The ETR (CIT), however, may be informative, particularly providing that any material variations are adequately and fairly explained.

Presentation: clarity, understandability

Information should be made available in a manner that is understandable and accessible to stakeholders. This covers everything from publication method (e.g. public online report) to language; visual format; use of graphic aids, such as tables and figures; appendices clarifying terms; and indices showing on which page each indicator or piece of information can be found (e.g. GRI index as prescribed by the standards).

For easy access and user-friendliness, the EU uses a practical rule of "maximum one 'click' out of the report" to indicate that information referred to in non-financial reporting should be achieved directly through clicking a hyperlink in the report (European Commission, 2019, p. 6). For example, the common practice of referring to financial statements for the income taxes paid figure in the GRI index would be adequate if a direct hyperlink leading to the correct page in the financial statements was provided in the version published online. However, simply stating that the information is available in the annual report without even indicating a specific page number would not fulfil the condition.

Presenting quantitative information, such as taxes by country or by type, is most often done in a table or chart format, as this is clear and concise, as well as visually appealing. An example of a tax footprint, distinguishing between taxes borne and collected, can be found in Figure 5.2. (Note: Figures 5.2–5.4 are composed for illustration purposes, and the numbers do not reflect any company's actual performance.)

Additionally, given that CIT is of particular interest from the tax avoidance point of view, a chart presenting the year-to-year trend with profit and tax rate could be advisable (example in Figure 5.3).

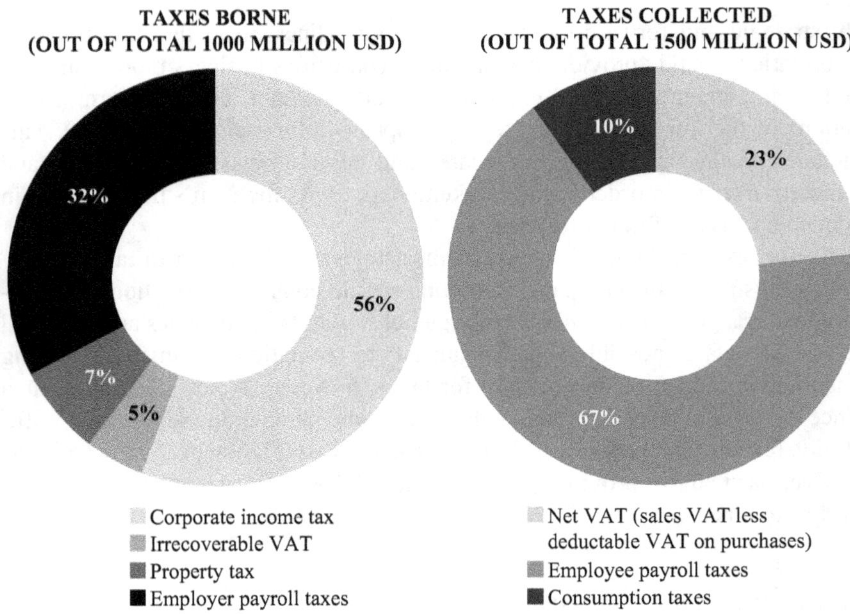

Figure 5.2 Tax footprint charts

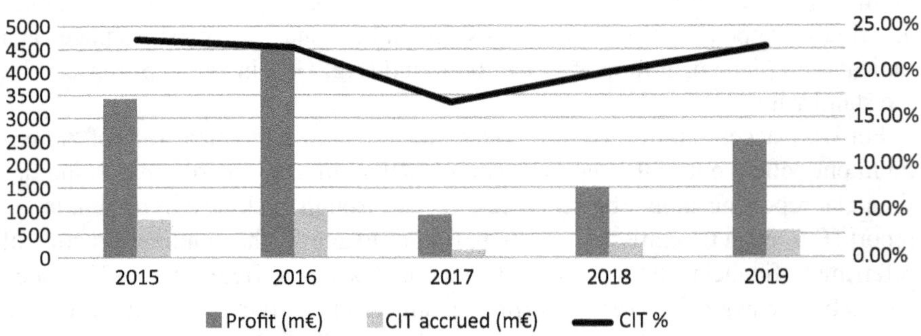

Figure 5.3 CIT year-to-year trend chart

Given that the GRI topic-specific Standard on Tax and Payments to Governments draft includes both CIT accrued (i.e. recorded in book-keeping) and paid (i.e. on cash basis), a graph showing their reconciliation could be useful (example in Figure 5.4). Any material exceptional items – e.g. tax expense adjustments or payments related to re-assessments by tax authorities – should be clearly specified and/or presented separately and additional information given on each case.

Some companies include a list of key terms as part of their reporting – for example, defining the meaning of different tax rates and distinguishing between

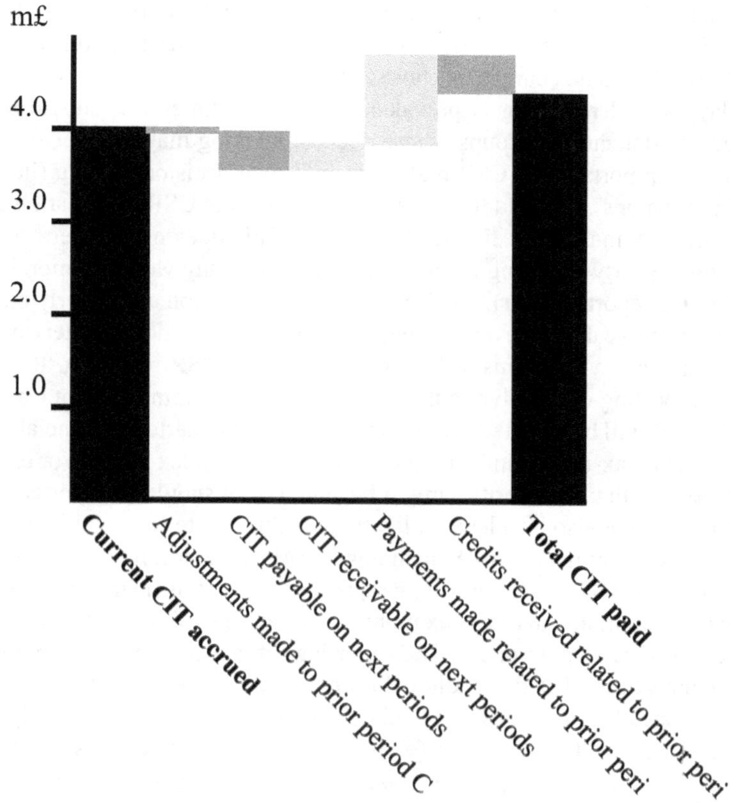

Figure 5.4 Reconciliation of CIT accrued and paid

taxes borne and collected. This practice is useful as tax matters are complicated, and being precise about terms and definitions helps avoid misinterpretation.

Explanations for significant variations in trends (e.g. changes in effective corporate tax rates or in composition of tax footprint) should be explained with sufficient detail (e.g. where applicable, references to tax law changes in different countries, impact of any non-recurring items or impact of specific events or market conditions to profitability in different countries). Again, this could benefit the reporting organisation so that any potentially negative effects of misinterpretations would be avoided.

Timing of reporting: timeliness

In the IFRS Conceptual Framework, timeliness means that information is available to decision makers in time to be capable of influencing their decisions (Deloitte, 2018). As far as CSR reporting is voluntary, there are no set deadlines for publishing the report. Commonly, separate CSR reports have been published after financial reporting. Integrated reports contain both financial and CSR information and may be published timelier due to pressures to publish financial results. Initially, some companies chose to report on CSR results every two years, but today, annual reporting is prevalent. Evaluating timeliness should address the needs of stakeholder groups whose decision making may be affected. Given the growing importance of CSR matters to informed decision making (including financial decisions), it would follow that the provision of CSR information should be as timely as mandatory financial reporting. This does not concern only the timing when yearly reporting is published (i.e. how many weeks or months after the end of the reporting year) but also the possible provision of quarterly information during the year. However, the publication of information at intervals more frequent than one year seems to be a rare practice in CSR reporting. It is likely that CSR reporting will evolve so that it becomes more common that at least some key indicators will be reported, for instance, along with quarterly financial results. With respect to tax-related information, major changes in tax strategy or exposure to arguments with tax authorities might be matters that should be reported as they occur (there might also be a legal obligation for this due to financial impacts).

The EU Accounting Directive, including non-financial information, determines that the non-financial statement is either prepared as part of financial reporting or in a separate report no later than six months after the end of the financial year. The proposed EU directive for public CbC reporting sets a deadline of 12 months after the financial year end. This deadline does not really support timeliness. In comparison, financial results of MNEs tend to be published more quickly, only weeks after the end of the financial year (earlier than legal deadlines prescribe) due to pressures from investors and other stakeholders. Of the tax-specific disclosures, the UK Finance Act requires the tax strategy document to be published for the first time before the end of the financial year in which the company has become qualified to publish it. After that, an updated document should be issued not more than 15 months after the publication of the latest version.

Cost constraint

In the IFRS conceptual framework, the benefit of providing the information needs to justify the cost of providing and using the information. In CSR reporting, this would mean that resources should be directed towards providing material information (considering the relative importance of different material topics). Additionally, organisations cannot in all cases provide 100% accurate information due to excessive costs related to data collection or calculation. In those circumstances, information provided would still need to be materially correct so that users are not misinformed. In the sphere of tax reporting, MNEs are required to report taxes by country to tax authorities, which means that the information would be available for public CSR reporting without additional costs for collection.

Summary of different quality aspects

The emphasis on reliability, verification and comparability is supported by EY's 2017 survey on one stakeholder group's investors' views on the usefulness of non-financial reporting. According to EY's survey, appreciation of CSR reporting has risen: in 2017, only 16% thought that non-financial information was not material and has no financial impact compared to 60% in 2013. However, demand for the quality of information has also increased: in 2017, 42% of respondents criticised the lack of consistency, availability and verification of non-financial information, as well as the limited possibilities to compare non-financial measures across companies. In 2013, only 20% raised these concerns. Investors, therefore, view the lack of comparable information and limited consistency, availability and verification as equally important issues preventing them from considering non-financial issues in decision making (EY, 2017).

It is important to note that transparency cannot be understood simply in terms of the volume of data available, but its quality aspects (relevance, reliability, comparability, verification) are crucial if it is to be useful for stakeholders' decision making. Requiring companies to produce data that is not relevant to any users or not reliable enough for decision making does not achieve much and can have adverse impacts. As Oats and Tuck (2019, p. 566) note, "Transparency is a costly regulatory strategy, not only for the providers of the information but also for those required to process it". Excessive reporting requirements put a strain on companies, and these increased administration costs (including internal work hours, as well as possibly external verification) are ultimately transferred to the price of the goods and services they sell. Additionally, reporting requirements put strain on authorities that need to monitor the provision of information and process the information. In Chapter 3, we discussed information overload and the limits to processing information. Advances in technology, such as AI, may remedy the problem in the near future (discussed in detail later in this chapter). For the time being, however, excessive information could, in fact, obscure company activities (Oats & Tuck, 2019, p. 567), and material information could be lost. Hence guaranteeing the provision of quality information that is relevant as well as reliable, accurate and comparable is crucial for real transparency. In the next part, we look at some safeguards against companies lacking accountability in guaranteeing such quality information.

5.2.2 Accountability and tax transparency

According to Adams (2008, p. 366), accountability is unlikely to be achieved in the absence of (1) robust stakeholder engagement, (2) widely accepted reporting guidelines, (3) assurance guidelines, (4) legislation and (5) penalties for non-compliance.

Firstly, engaging stakeholders is crucial in ascertaining that information provided is useful and that all material information is provided to different stakeholders. Secondly, widely accepted reporting guidelines would facilitate comparisons either across companies (when different companies report the same information and the indicators are calculated according to the same principles) or across years (when firms follow the same reporting pattern consistently). Thirdly, requirement for external assurance would improve the reliability of information reported and set guidelines for verifiers would further enhance and standardise the quality of verification (for example, through setting the scope requirement for external verification). Finally, legislation and penalties for non-compliance are the ultimate guarantors for spreading the reporting if pressures from stakeholders do not motivate companies to report voluntarily.

We can already see developments that are addressing these concerns. For instance, the draft of GRI's topic-specific standard on Tax and Payments to Governments presented earlier responds to the need for stakeholder engagement and widely accepted reporting guidelines. In Chapter 1, we presented the legislative initiatives aimed at advancing tax-related reporting. However, the present legislative requirements are limited in scope, either by field of industry (e.g. EITI) or country (UK tax strategy disclosure requirement) and usually only apply to public interest entities or large entities. Regarding sanctions for non-compliance, the EU Accounting Directive leaves it to member states to determine sanctions for non-compliance with the requirement for providing non-financial information in the national legislation. The UK Finance Act includes a fine to the head of group of £7,500 if a tax strategy report is prepared late (up to six months after the end of the financial year) and a further £7,500 each subsequent month until the report is published.

Assurance of tax-related information is voluntary if it is not part of official financial reporting subject to legal audit requirements or country-specific requirements (e.g. Grenelle Act in France requiring the reporting of certain CSR information and its verification). There exist no specific assurance guidelines for tax-related reporting. However, if CSR information is externally verified (and tax-related information is part of it), the most frequently applied standard by professional accountants is ISAE3000. ISAE3000 is the standard designed for engagements other than audits or reviews of historical financial information covered by ISAs (International Standards on Auditing) or ISREs (International Standard on Review Engagements, i.e. other than financial statement audits). It sets the general requirements for ethical conduct, quality controls, engagement acceptance, continuance and terms, planning and execution of the engagement, evidence and documentation, as well as preparing the report. The AA1000AS assurance standard issued by the non-profit organisation AccountAbility is less frequently used and more often referred to by assurers from outside the accounting profession (Simnett, 2012). Canning, O'Dwyer and Georgakopoulos (2019) have examined how assurers (both with an accounting and non-accounting background) apply the concept of materiality in sustainability reporting assurance. They consider if the reporting organisation had identified all material stakeholders, reported on all material topics and determined if the information audited was free of material error. Hence external assurance addresses not only the accuracy or reliability of information (i.e. free from material error) but also the aspects of completeness (reporting on all material topics) and the fundamental principle of stakeholder engagement (identification of all material stakeholders). Although generally voluntary (some national exceptions aside), external verification of CSR reports has become more common: according to KPMG's 2017 survey, assurance of CSR data more than doubled amongst the world's largest 250 companies by revenue between 2005–2017, reaching 67% of reports in 2017. Assurance has also been steadily rising amongst the 100 largest companies per country, increasing to 45% in 2017 from 33% in 2005 (KPMG, 2017, p. 26). Our empirical research results presented in Chapter 4 similarly show an incline in the number of reports externally verified. This indicates that companies see value in promoting the reliability of the CSR information they provide to make it more useful to stakeholders.

As for existing audit requirements, the EU Accounting Directive containing the requirement for non-financial disclosures demands that reporting organisations' auditor checks that the report has been provided, but it is up to member states' discretion if they require the information to be verified in the national legislation implementing the directive. The CRD IV impacting financial institutions requires the CbC reporting (including tax on profit figures) to be audited. For example, Royal Bank of Scotland (RBS), subject to the directive, publishes annual auditor statements on its CbC reporting as an appendix to its annual report and accounts (to which its CSR reporting has been integrated since 2016) but does not directly refer to the report in the GRI content (201-1), although that would be relevant information.

In sum, to best advance tax transparency, reporting requirements should focus on quality of information as opposed to simply making more data available. Information should be useful for stakeholders' decision making – i.e. relevant, reliable, comparable and timely. The public CbC reporting requirements by EU or GRI standards are a welcome development as they standardise reporting and facilitate comparability both on a year-to-year basis, as well as amongst different companies. The proposed EU public CbC reporting directive focuses on CIT. As this is the most receptive tax type to aggressive avoidance strategies, this focus is backed up by the relevance criteria. Additionally, the proposed directive includes a requirement for external audit, which has a positive impact on guaranteeing reliability and accuracy of information. Given the cost constraints that companies face and the limits to users' information processing capabilities, prioritising reporting requirements is reasonable. The draft of a new GRI topic-specific standard aims at providing a fuller picture of companies' tax footprints, including other tax types in addition to CIT as optional reporting under Disclosure 5. Nonetheless, it should be noted that the standard does not require reporting unless the topic is deemed relevant in the materiality assessment, considering impacts and stakeholders' information needs.

5.2.3 CbC reporting – critique and benefits

We have argued that the disclosure of country-specific information, particularly CIT, contributes positively to global tax transparency. However, the possible drawbacks should also be recognised and analysed. In relation to the concept of cost restraint, we have noted the direct costs related to preparing CbC and tax footprint reporting. However, CbC reporting has been criticised for causing companies indirect costs as well. Critics are concerned that even non-public disclosures violate national laws on tax secrecy when information would be disclosed to foreign tax authorities and foresaw this leading to tax-related distributional conflicts when different countries' tax authorities would seek to maximise their revenue (Evers, Meier & Spengel, 2016, p. 10). The OECD disclosure requirements for tax authorities have been established nonetheless.

Criticisms raised against public CbC reporting are most often related to competitive disadvantages caused by confidential information being made public. For example, the EU proposed public CbC requirement leaves "small" MNEs outside its scope; hence, it could be seen as giving them an unfair advantage. Additionally, companies inside the EU member states would face a significant disadvantage compared to companies based in other countries without public disclosure requirements. Furthermore, users' abilities to adequately understand and interpret information have been questioned: as international tax laws are highly complex, correctly processing the information would require profound knowledge of the subject and the MNEs allocation of functions and risks (Evers, Meier & Spengel, 2016, p. 10); otherwise, users might jump to false conclusions about, for instance, low tax payments.

To illustrate, these concerns are reflected in the sustainability reporting of Outotec, a Finnish company offering services and technology to the mining, metal, energy and chemical industries. The company provides this explanation for not disclosing country-specific tax information: "Outotec engages in large projects, however there may be only one project ongoing in a country. Due to the confidential nature of the information and the varying quantities of projects worldwide we cannot disclose country specific financial information" (Outotec, 2017, p. 10). In addition, the company points out that as the destinations of sales typically do not correspond with the places in which value is created, where income has to be reported and taxes paid, providing country-specific data would not give a comprehensive picture of the fairness of the company's tax distribution (Outotec, 2017, p. 10). This example illustrates both the confidentiality consideration and the concern that users might misinterpret information due to its complex nature. Regarding the former, companies seem to be impacted differently, as some have chosen to disclose the information voluntary for years without fearing competitive disadvantages. This has been demonstrated by empirical research: "Certain studies demonstrate that MNEs hide geographic earnings out of fear of revealing proprietary information, while other research shows that they are not motivated by this concern" (Cockfield & MacArthur, 2015, p. 647). Given the differences between companies' activities, this result is unsurprising. For example, it is logical that companies pursuing project-based business (such as Outotec) do not wish to disclose data that would effectively offer information on the profitability of individual projects. Disclosure requirements should take this into account, establishing a method for explaining omissions if they can be reliably justified based on business secrets. However, this possibility should not be exploited by companies without substantial reasons so that faithful representation is secured. Regarding the second consideration, the complex nature of information, companies can do much by providing adequate explanation enabling better analysis and interpretation. Giving the necessary information would hardly in all cases mean disclosing trade secrets.

To summarise, we argue that the benefits of transparent tax reporting outweigh the drawbacks. The OECD CbC reporting requirements have already improved tax authorities' capabilities to perform better risk analysis concerning, for example, transfer-pricing audits, and to better discern arm's-length values through the availability of aggregated information (Cockfield & MacArthur, 2015, p. 640). However, tax authorities are not the only stakeholder group that deserves the right to transparent information to aid their decision making. Public disclosure of relevant and high-quality tax information, including strategy and CbC data, can, for example, assist investors in risk assessments and the media in providing accurate information in its coverage of the topic. Making companies accountable for reporting is also thought to discourage aggressive tax avoidance strategies, as reporting (if prepared in accordance with the quality criteria presented earlier) would reveal significant arrangements in tax havens or other significant minimisation strategies.

5.3 CSR and tax transparency in the age of AI

AI is not a new phenomenon, but recent technological breakthroughs in computing speed, components and more efficient algorithms facilitate AI entrance into new fields. AI term is "frequently applied to the project of developing systems endowed with the intellectual processes characteristic of humans, such as the ability to reason, discover meaning, generalize, or learn from past experience" (Copeland, 2018, p. 1). Such activities and/or processes are very multidisciplinary, including engineering, statistics, linguistics, logic and computer science (Copeland, 2018). Machine learning in its turn is a subset of AI. AI should not be understood as replacing humans but the augmentation of human capabilities.

AI is best at dealing with large quantities of data. It helps equipped sieve through vast quantities of information and find only which is relevant. AI can potentially alleviate the problem of information overload discussed in Chapter 4. While AI use in medicine, retail and transport is well publicised, further research is needed on AI application in CSR and tax reporting. We further explore AI implications on CSR and tax functions from a multiple stakeholder perspective and evaluate its impact on tax transparency by the companies.

5.3.1 CSR in the light of AI

There has been a surge in voluntary CSR standards in recent years, with companies expected to disclose an increasing volume of information. Most notably, companies are expected to report on how they engage with the UN Sustainable Development

Goals (SDGs) in their corporate planning. SDGs have been incorporated into GRI's publication "Corporate Reporting: A Practical Guide". Moreover, companies are expected to publish various climate-change-addressing disclosures, such as Task Force of Climate-Related Reporting (TCFD, 2019) consistent reports.

AI can assist in processing the high volume of information required to compile a CSR report. It can be utilised to reduce human bias in value measurement, to assist in materiality tests and to identify integration points of corporate strategy and various CSR initiatives. Comparing a company's data against global standards can be done faster and easier with the help of AI (Al Naqvi, 2019). AI has already been used to achieve changes in, for example, efficiency and emissions reductions, and to innovate new products and services (Riffle, 2017).

Eventually, the use of AI itself needs to be addressed as part of CSR reporting since it is an ethically charged issue. For instance, Intel released its public policy principles for developing AI. AI is subject to the bias of the creator (what are the rules of the algorithm that AI runs on) and machine bias whereby AI learns from past data that may not be sufficient or inclusive – e.g. of minorities, children and other groups. AI-assisted decisions should be weighted on the basis of short-term profits against sustainable ethical values (Felländer, 2018). The General Data Protection Regulation (EU) 2016/679 (GDPR) strengthens consumers' access to data and requires transparency of automated-assisted decisions, so this needs to be addressed when designing AI systems. AI-assisted systems can be utilised by stakeholders for automatically finding flaws and analysing reports' sentiment and tone. Hence the firm producing CSR reports shall be aware of the AI capabilities of stakeholders – e.g. financial analysist and fund managers.

5.3.2 What AI means for different tax stakeholders

AI and tax authorities

Tax authorities serve two main functions: to manage tax compliance and to provide services and education to taxpayers. According to the Center for Public Impact (2018) report, tax authorities have always been at the forefront of deploying analytics and using predictive risk models to detect tax avoidance. So the adoption of AI is important for predictive and prescriptive analytics. Predictive analytics serve to identify possible tax-related problems and solutions for tax authorities, while prescriptive analytics model the impact of actions on tax payers. AI systems help integrate both predictive and prescriptive analytics and are already in use in Australia, Norway and the UK. Using mature AI systems would also mean substantial labour cost savings for the tax authorities that historically had to employ a seasonal workforce for the end of the tax year period. The Center for Public Impact (2018) report noted that tax authorities were unwilling to share their models' weights and logic in fear that users may game the system.

There are several examples of AI providing services and education to taxpayers. The Swedish Tax Agency utilised AI for improving customer service by introducing a digital employee, the chatbot "Skatti", that helps with answering people's questions about their tax returns. Skatti handled over 200,000 individual queries averaging 15,000 chats per month (AI Innovation of Sweden, 2019). The ultimate goal is to fight crime and make it difficult for people to avoid their fiscal duties. In the UK, HMRC employs AI for automating repetitive tasks and achieved a goal of ten million automated processes by the end of 2018 on tasks as varied as contact handling, casework decision making and helping customers through effective self-service (Holl, 2017). In Spring 2019, The Finnish Tax Administration published ethical principles for the use of artificial intelligence. Principles state that AI only uses reliable data; a human is always responsible for AI operations; AI follows laws and regulations, and Finnish Tax Administration takes part in public discussion on responsible and ethical AI applications. Additionally, principles provide an explanation "whether the AI is allowed to make independent decisions or whether it just generates suggestions to tax officials is determined separately for each solution" (Finnish Tax Administration, 2019). Hereafter, it would be beneficial to find out how tax authorities employ AI for combatting tax avoidance by MNEs.

Taking into consideration the resources tax authorities invest into developing AI capabilities in the future, we may expect high rates of tax avoidance detection. It should also promote higher rates of pre-emptive voluntarily tax transparency disclosures; for once information is open, there should be no need for further investigation. While GDPR (2016) advocates against AI-assisted profiling of individuals, it allows it for tax evasion purposes (GDPR article 71):

> However, decision-making based on such processing, including profiling, should be allowed where expressly authorised by Union or Member State law to which the controller is subject, including for fraud and tax-evasion monitoring and prevention purposes conducted in accordance with the regulations, standards and recommendations of Union institutions or national oversight bodies and to ensure the security and reliability of a service provided by the controller, or necessary for the entering or performance of a contract between the data subject and a controller, or when the data subject has given his or her explicit consent.

In the future, tax authorities may use AI for real-time data reports, real-time audits and sharing information across borders (WTS Global, 2018). At the current stage of AI development, tax authorities may benefit only marginally due to the nature of tax avoidance detection skills because they

> (i) belong to the domain of cognitive non-routine tasks; (ii) engage powers of persuasion, judgement and common sense (including creative and social intelligence); (iii) take place in complex situations; and (iv) often require group work or face-to-face interactions with stakeholders (clients, employees of tax authorities, judges, etc.).
>
> (Kuźniacki, 2019, p. 8)

Similarly, a study by WTS Global (2018) titled "Getting Ready for the Future of the Tax Function" concludes that the implementation of AI applications for tax purposes is still in its infancy.

AI and companies

AI could mean labour cost savings for companies where AI replaces manual tax classification tasks – e.g. classification of deductible non-deductible expenses, recurring and non-recurring and perform tax classification problems (Xing, 2019). Deloitte's (2017) report on AI in tax lists compliance facilitation as one of the biggest advantages of using AI, especially in the light of higher external expectations of complying with OECD BEPS and the Common Reporting Standard (an information standard for the Automatic Exchange of Information (AEOI) regarding bank accounts on a global level, between tax authorities)

The WTS Global (2018) report further lists application of AI in internal control systems for tax and new regulations. Some countries, such as Australia and Brazil, require companies to implement data interfaces for electronic filling of tax returns, including extensive data access for local tax authorities. In the short-term, AI can help companies with error analysis, compliance security and cost reduction (WTS Global, 2018). As companies become mature in digitalisation in the long-term, use of AI and digitalisation will help firms to have a stronger focus on the global tax strategy.

Summary

Reporting about tax issues in CSR reporting has become more common during recent years. This development is likely to accelerate due to legislative initiatives (particularly the EU-proposed directive on CbC reporting), as well as voluntary reporting standards (GRI topic-specific standard on tax and payments to governments). The variation amongst companies is currently large: a few companies report extensively, covering many aspects of the topic, but many do not discuss tax issues at all under the umbrella of CSR. However, the view that paying taxes is part of responsible corporate citizenship can be found in many reports, which suggests companies believe that tax issues do have a place as part of CSR. The arguments by media, governments and civil society organisations on the significance of tax payments to societies support this view. Furthermore, there is a growing body of research on tax matters as part of CSR. We have shown how CSR theories can be applied to explaining the emergence and spread of tax reporting. The attention by the media, the public and the authorities through revelations on tax avoidance strategies has increased the demand for tax-related information. At the same time, reputational and financial risks for companies engaging in aggressive tax minimisation have increased.

In the future, it will be crucial to focus on the quality aspects of tax information, as opposed to simply prescribing more data to be reported. This applies to legislators, CSR reporting standard-setters and reporting companies. Useful information is first and foremost relevant to stakeholders and needs to be reliable and comparable to enable good decision making. Standard-setters and legislators should aim for aligning their reporting requirements as far as feasible to avoid excessive administrative burden on companies. The use of AI can assist both in producing the data and processing it, alleviating reporters' compliance costs, as well as users' information overload. The impacts of the application of AI also offers interesting avenues for future research.

Given the recent and forthcoming developments, future research on the impacts of CbC tax reporting would be welcome. Additionally, reasons behind companies' decision to voluntarily report or their reluctance to disclose information should be explored so that considerations related to reputation management on the one hand and possible competitive disadvantages and other proprietary costs on the other could be more reliably captured. Moreover, more research applying economic theories is needed to identify the impact of more transparent tax reporting on the cost of capital and corporate governance. Inclusion of tax matters in the agent-principle contracts is also of interest.

We may expect tax transparency to transition to mainstream CSR reporting, and companies need to be prepared for it. By providing tax transparency reporting, companies can present their view on tax transparency as part of responsible corporate citizenship. Companies have an opportunity to explain why they view tax transparency as material component of their CSR and share long-term perspectives on the impact of their tax policies on societies. Current focus on isolated income tax figures could be complemented by providing more comprehensive information on total tax contribution and CbC reporting. At the same, we recognise that the field of tax transparency is continuously changing, and there is a need for new skills and capabilities amongst CSR and tax professionals, as well as assurers of tax transparency reporting. Similarly, stakeholders need information on what to consider as good practice and what to look for in these reports. In addition to presenting forthcoming developments in reporting frameworks, this book has summarised important quality considerations and provided examples of existing good practices in order to advance transparent tax reporting.

Notes

1 Reportable segments are operating segments or aggregations of operating segments that meet specified criteria: [IFRS 8.13] Its reported revenue, from both external customers and intersegment sales or transfers, is 10% or more of the combined revenue, internal and external, of all operating segments, or the absolute measure of its reported profit or loss is 10% or more of the greater, in absolute amount, of (1) the combined reported profit of all operating segments that did not report a loss and (2) the combined reported loss of all operating segments that reported a loss, or its assets are 10% or more of the combined assets of all operating segments.

2 A chatbot is an AI program that simulates interactive human conversation by using key pre-calculated user phrases and auditory or text-based signals. Chatbots are frequently used for basic customer service and marketing systems that frequent social networking hubs and instant messaging clients. They are also often included in operating systems as intelligent virtual assistants (Technopedia, 2019).

References

Adams, C. A., 2008, 'A Commentary on: Corporate Social Responsibility Reporting and Reputation Risk Management', *Accounting, Auditing & Accountability Journal*, 21 (3), pp. 365–370.

AI Innovation of Sweden, 2019, 'Artificial Intelligence Improves the Swedish Tax Agency's Customer Service', Available at www.ai.se/en/news/artificial-intelligence-improves-swedish-tax-agencys-customer-service. Accessed 10/06/2019.

Al Naqvi, 2019, 'How AI and Robotics Can Transform CSR', *Ethical Corporation*. Available at www.ethicalcorp.com/how-ai-and-robotics-can-transform-csr. Accessed 29/05/2019.

Canning, M., O'Dwyer, B. and Georgakopoulos, G., 2019, 'Processes of Auditability in Sustainability Assurance: The Case of Materiality Construction', *Accounting and Business Research*, 49 (1), pp. 1–27.

Centre for Public Impact, 2018, 'Artificial Intelligence in Taxation: A Case Study on the Use of AI in Government', Available at https://resources.centreforpublicimpact.org/production/2019/01/CPI-AI-Case-Study-Taxation.pdf. Accessed 30/05/2019.

Cockfield, A. and MacArthur, C., 2015, 'Country-by-Country Reporting and Commercial Confidentiality', *Canadian Tax Journal/Revue Fiscale Canadienne*, 63 (3), pp. 627–660.

Copeland, B. J., 2018, 'Artificial Intelligence (Last updated 3 May 2018)', Available at www.britannica.com/technology/artificial-intelligence. Accessed 20/05/2019.

Deloitte, 2017, 'Artificial Intelligence-Entering the World of Tax', Available at www2.deloitte.com/content/dam/Deloitte/global/Documents/Tax/dttl-tax-artificial-intelligence-in-tax.pdf. Accessed 10/06/2019.

Deloitte, 2018, 'Conceptual Framework for Financial Reporting 2018', Available at https://www.iasplus.com/en/standards/other/framework. Accessed 8.7.2018.

Deutsche Post DHL Group, 'Corporate Responsibility Report 2017', Available at www.dpdhl.com/content/dam/dpdhl/en/media-center/responsibility/dpdhl-corporate-responsibility-report-2017.pdf. Accessed 03/08/2018.

Diageo plc, 'Sustainability & Responsibility Performance Addendum to the Annual Report 2015', Available at www.diageo.com/PR1346/aws/media/1440/diageo_sr_perf_addendum_2015.pdf. Accessed 28/06/2019.

European Commission, 2017, 'Communication from the Commission: Guidelines on Non-Financial Reporting (Methodology for Reporting Non-Financial Information)', *2017/C 215/01*. Available at https://eur-lex.europa.eu/legal-content/EN/TXT/?uri=CELEX:52017XC0705(01). Accessed 27/06/2019.

European Commission, 2019, 'Guidelines on Reporting Climate-Related Information', Available at http://ec.europa.eu/finance/docs/policy/190618-climate-related-information-reporting-guidelines_en.pdf. Accessed 22/06/2019.

Evers, M. T., Meier, I. and Spengel, C., 2016, 'Country-by-Country Reporting: Tension between Transparency and Tax Planning', Discussion Paper No. 17-008. ZEW Zentrum für Europäische Wirtshaftsforschung GmbH. Available at http://ftp.zew.de/pub/zew-docs/dp/dp17008.pdf. Accessed 24/06/2019.

EY, 2017, 'Is Your Nonfinancial Performance Revealing the True Value of Your Business to Investors?', Available at www.ey.com/Publication/vwLUAssets/EY_-_Nonfinancial_performance_may_influence_investors/$FILE/ey-nonfinancial-performance-may-influence-investors.pdf. Accessed 10/08/2018.

Felländer, A., 2018, 'AI Sustainability: A New Form of CSR', *Tinius Trust*. Available at https://tinius.com/2018/01/15/ai-sustainability-a-new-form-of-csr/. Accessed 29/05/2019.

Finnish Tax Administration, 2019, 'Finnish Tax Administration's Ethical Principles for AI', Available at www.vero.fi/en/About-us/finnish-tax-administration/operations/responsibility/finnish-tax-administrations-ethical-principles-for-ai/. Accessed 29/06/2019.

GDPR, 2016, 'Regulation (EU) 2016/679 of the European Parliament and of the Council of 27 April 2016 on the Protection of Natural Persons with Regard to the Processing of Personal Data and on the Free Movement of Such Data, and Repealing Directive 95/46/EC (General Data Protection Regulation)', Available at https://eur-lex.europa.eu/legal-content/EN/TXT/PDF/?uri=CELEX:32016R0679&from=EN. Accessed 29/05/2019.

GlaxoSmithKline plc (GSK), 'Responsible Business Supplement 2016', Available at www.gsk.com/media/3610/responsible-business-supplement-2016.pdf. Accessed 28/06/2019.

GRI, 2016, 'GRI Standards, GRI-101 Foundation 2016', Available at www.globalreporting.org/standards/gri-standards-download-center/. Accessed 18/05/2017.

GRI, 2019a, 'Exposure Draft: Tax & Payments to Governments Standard', Available at www.globalreporting.org/standards/media/2213/exposure-draft-standard-for-tax-and-payments-to-governments-with-survey-questions.pdf. Accessed 10/06/2019.

GRI, 2019b, 'Integrating the SDGs Into Corporate Reporting: A Practical Guide', Available at www.globalreporting.org/resourcelibrary/GRI_UNGC_Reporting-on-SDGs_Practical_Guide.pdf. Accessed 10/06/2019.

Holl, M., 2017, 'Artificial Intelligence and Machine Learning: Exploring the Possibilities', Available at https://hmrcdigital.blog.gov.uk/2017/07/17/artificial-intelligence-and-machine-learning-exploring-the-possibilities/. Accessed 09/06/2019.

IFRS 8, 2018, 'Operating Segments', Available at www.iasplus.com/en/standards/ifrs/ifrs8. Accessed 12/06/2019.

IFRS Foundation, 2018, 'Conceptual Framework for Financial Reporting', *IFRS Conceptual Framework Project Summary*. March. Available at www.ifrs.org/-/media/project/conceptual-framework/fact-sheet-project-summary-and-feedback-statement/conceptual-framework-project-summary.pdf. Accessed 09/06/2019.

Intel, 2017, 'Artificial Intelligence the Public Policy Opportunity', Available at https://blogs.intel.com/policy/files/2017/10/Intel-Artificial-Intelligence-Public-Policy-White-Paper-2017.pdf. Accessed 26/05/2019.

Intel Corporation, 'Corporate Responsibility at Intel, 2017–2018 Report', Available at https://csrreportbuilder.intel.com/PDFfiles/CSR-2017_Full-Report.pdf. Accessed 04/08/2018.

KPMG, 2017, 'The Road Ahead: The KPMG Survey of Corporate Responsibility Reporting 2017', Available at https://assets.kpmg/content/dam/kpmg/be/pdf/2017/kpmg-survey-of-corporate-responsibility-reporting-2017.pdf. Accessed 20/06/2019.

Kuźniacki, B., 2019, 'The Marriage of Artificial Intelligence and Tax Law: Past, Present, and Future (January 27, 2019)', Available at http://dx.doi.org/10.2139/ssrn.3323867. Accessed 20/05/2019.

Neste Oyj, 'Annual Report 2016: Section 2 Sustainability', Available at https://ir-service.appspot.com/view/ahBzfmlyLXNlcnZpY2UtaHJkchsLEg5GaWxlQXR0YWNobWVudBiAgJDA85KXCAw?language_no=0. Accessed 28/06/2019.

Nordea Bank AB, 'Sustainability Report 2016', Available at www.nordea.com/Images/37-247009/Nordea_Sustainability_Report_2017_printable.pdf. Accessed 13/01/2019.

Nordea Bank AB, 'Sustainability Report 2017', Available at www.nordea.com/Images/33-247009/Nordea_Sustainability_Report_2017_printable.pdf. Accessed 21/07/2018.

Oats, L. and Tuck, P., 2019, 'Corporate Tax Avoidance: Is Tax Transparency the Solution?', *Accounting and Business Research*, 49 (5), pp. 565–583.

Outotec, 'Outotec Sustainability Report 2017: Refining Data for Sustainability', Available at www.outotec.com/sustainability-report/2017/. Accessed 21/07/2018.

Reckitt Benckiser Group plc, 'Sustainability Report 2017', Available at www.rb.com/media/3353/rb-sustainability-report-2017.pdf. Accessed 15/01/2019.

Riffle, C., 2017, 'What Artificial Intelligence Means for Sustainability', Available at www.greenbiz.com/article/what-artificial-intelligence-means-sustainability. Accessed 26/05/2019.

Simnett, R., 2012, 'Assurance of Sustainability Reports: Revision of ISAE 3000 and Associated Research Opportunities', *Sustainability Accounting, Management and Policy Journal*, 3, pp. 89–98.

TCFD, 2019, 'The Task Force on Climate-Related Financial Disclosures (TCFD)', Available at www.fsb-tcfd.org/. Accessed 29/05/2019.

Technopedia, 2019, 'Chatbot Definition', Available at www.techopedia.com/definition/16366/chatterbot. Accessed 10/07/2019.

WPP, 'Sustainability Report 2016/2017', Available at https://sites.wpp.com/sustainability reports/2016/downloads/. Accessed 01/07/2018.

WTS Global, 2018, 'Getting Ready for the Future of the Tax Function: Digital Tax Maturity and AI Readiness', *WTS Study*. Available at www.wts.com/wts.de/insights/kuenstliche-intelligenz/wtsai_getting-ready-for-the-future-of-the-tax-function.pdf. Accessed 20/05/2019.

Xing, P., 2019, 'Machine Learning for Tax', Available at https://medium.com/data driveninvestor/machine-learning-for-tax-f49694963e35. Accessed 30/05/2019.

Index

For Product Safety Concerns and Information please contact our EU representative GPSR@taylorandfrancis.com
Taylor & Francis Verlag GmbH, Kaufingerstraße 24, 80331 München, Germany

www.ingramcontent.com/pod-product-compliance
Lightning Source LLC
LaVergne TN
LVHW021111300926
849160LV00009B/695

* 9 7 8 1 0 3 2 1 7 5 7 1 3 *